WITCHES
SLUTS
FEMINISTS

WITCHES
SLUTS
FEMINISTS

CONJURING THE SEX POSITIVE

KRISTEN J. SOLLÉE

Illustrations by Coz Conover

ThreeL Media | Berkeley

Published by
ThreeL Media | Stone Bridge Press
P. O. Box 8208, Berkeley, CA 94707
www.threelmedia.com
© 2017 Kristen J. Sollée

Printed in the United States of America.

p-ISBN: 978-0-9964852-7-2
e-ISBN: 978-0-9964852-8-9

CONTENTS

INTRODUCTION

Maleficent was my first childhood crush. I was hypnotized by her stately horns, her pale green skin, and her extravagant eyes. I had no love for *Sleeping Beauty*'s heroine, Princess Aurora. She was too perfect, too un-relatable. But Maleficent? I could appreciate anger, frustration, rejection, and the raw expression of emotion all rolled into a roiling grand dame.

Back then I didn't realize just how much Maleficent's character reified harmful stereotypes about witches and women—I was too busy crafting my black cape out of bedsheets. This was long before Disney humanized her in the 2014 film *Maleficent*. This was when Maleficent lived up to her name, epitomizing chthonic forces and forbidden female power. She was the witch I wanted to be: a woman in control. A surviving video from my early years shows me with hands out, claw-like, brow furrowed, doing my best Maleficent impression. "On her sixteenth birthday, she shall prick her finger on the spindle of a spinning wheel—and die!" Somehow, I made it into adulthood without becoming a vengeful, horned villain.

Instead, I became a feminist.

Like many millennial women, I see a reclamation of female power in the witch, slut, and feminist identities. Each of these contested words conjure and counter a tortuous history of misogyny, and each in its own way can be emblematic of women overcoming oppression.

After a decade of exploring gender in contemporary music, art, and culture as a journalist, I started a sex-positive feminist website called *Slutist*. At the time, "slut" had recently been listed in *The Atlantic*'s "Worst Words" of 2012. The anti-victim-blaming SlutWalk movement was also gaining traction, and slut-shaming was becoming a frequently covered topic in the media. Playing upon the power of the word "slut" with both tongue-in-cheek revelry and dead seriousness, the site began as an outlet to address gender politics and female sexuality through op-eds, interviews, personal essays, and original artwork.

Before long, my lifelong fascination with the occult, alternative spiritual practices, and macabre aesthetics began to creep in. I found that dozens of the feminist writers, artists, and activists who contributed to the site felt as comfortable reclaiming or allying with the word "slut" as they did with the word "witch." Building community with those similarly entranced by transgressive sexuality and dark, dynamic, and misunderstood women, *Slutist* quickly spun into a leather- and lace-clad celebration of the witch-slut-feminist trifecta like Stevie Nicks sweeping the stage in 1976.*

After producing two critically acclaimed music, art, and burlesque festivals called "Legacy of the Witch" honoring the witch as a feminist icon, curating an interdisciplinary gallery show called "Witch Slut Are You?," and teaching multiple college courses on fourth-wave feminism and the feminist legacy of the witch at The New School, I knew it was time to examine the connections between witches, sluts, and feminists in a more codified form.

Witches, Sluts, Feminists: Conjuring the Sex Positive is an introduction to the sex-positive history of the witch. With a focus on sexual liberation, this book traces the lineage of "witch feminism" through art, film, music, fashion, literature, technology, religion, pop culture, and politics. It delves into reproductive

---

* For the record, the feminist Fleetwood Mac chanteuse has affirmed her love of witches and witchy fashion, but does not publicly identify as a witch.

rights, sexual pleasure, pornography, queer identity, body positivity, and sex work, and demonstrates why the "slut" is in many ways the "witch" of the twenty-first century.

Although many men and those on the masculine spectrum identify as witches and have historically been accused of witchcraft, this book specifically looks at the indivisible links between the witch, femininity, and womanhood—which includes trans women and anyone on the feminine spectrum—and the persecution women have faced as a result of their perceived connection with witchcraft. *Witches, Sluts, Feminists* thus explores the witch as an identity forced upon women, as an identity taken up freely by feminine individuals, and as an embodiment of those who practice witchcraft—an umbrella term for a variety of occult practices.

A commitment to intersectionality is non-negotiable when approaching any feminist herstory. I have endeavored to include the perspectives of a broad cross-section of feminists within these pages. I also recognize that many beloved feminist figures were/are flawed individuals. My inclusion of a particular activist, scholar, or artist does not reflect a rubber stamp of approval for their entire oeuvre, but merely affirms their role in the story of witches, sluts, and feminists.

The witch is not a Western, Christian invention by any stretch of the imagination. However, dominant narratives about witches and witchcraft in American history and popular culture are most informed by the Anglo-European, Christian lineage of the witch, which is why I chose it as the focus of this exploration. By juxtaposing leading scholarly research on witch persecutions in the US and Europe with pop *occult*ure analyses and interviews with feminists, activists, artists, academics, and practitioners of witchcraft, *Witches, Sluts, Feminists* connects the legendary character so many love to emulate or fear with revolutionary women of the past and present.

The structure of the book is cumulative. Initial chapters offer a condensed background on the witch from early civilization into medieval Europe and colonial America. Successive chapters build upon this foundation to show how gendered narratives about witches continue to impact and inform women in contemporary America. Each section undresses the witch in different ways through different methods, peeling back layers of misinformation and misogyny to chart her development from diabolical sorceress to symbol of feminist empowerment—and back.

At the end of the book, I've included interviews with self-identified witches to flesh out and humanize the modern-day witch. Following those interviews are my references. In addition, the official website www.witchesslutsfeminists.com offers multi-media content that expands upon the text.

I should now take a moment to discuss what this book isn't.

Witches, Sluts, Feminists is not a formal work of academic scholarship, although there are multiple academic sources central to my arguments.

Witches, Sluts, Feminists does not intend to promote one particular school of witchcraft—although there are a variety of practitioners interviewed within the book, and you may find a spell or two within these pages.

Witches, Sluts, Feminists is not an exhaustive catalogue of every notable witch from the beginning of time up to the present, nor does it address every important feminist issue under the sun. A few of my favorite sirens and subjects were left to melt on the cutting room floor. Brevity is the soul of witch, after all.

So what fresh spell is this little text?

I designed *Witches, Sluts, Feminists* to appeal to feminist scholars, historians, lawyers, artists, activists, occultists, and witchcraft practitioners as well as those unfamiliar with the cultural and political history of the witch—apart from what they've seen in mainstream media. This concise primer is an interdisciplinary take on a vast subject, spinning elements of a multi-faceted world in kaleidoscopic, new ways. Ideally, *Witches, Sluts, Feminists* will serve as a gateway drug, and which gateway you choose is up to you.

As I show throughout *Witches, Sluts, Feminists: Conjuring the Sex Positive*, the witch isn't necessarily who you think she is. The witch is undoubtedly the magical woman, the liberated woman, and the persecuted woman, but she can also be *everywoman*.

WITCHES, SLUTS, FEMINISTS

The witch is having a moment. Film and television are filled with tales of witches and otherworldly women, visual art and literature are plumbing the depths of pagan lore, and runways are replete with occult symbolism. For the newly anointed "generation witch," empowerment is central to her appeal.

Concurrently, feminism is a buzz word for the first time in decades. Pop stars are proclaiming their allegiance to gender equality on stage, actors are broaching political issues on the red carpet, and activists, politicians, educators, and everyday people alike are fighting for women's rights online, in the classroom, and in the streets.

In this cultural climate, the witch is increasingly viewed as a symbol of female power, but she is equally a symbol of female persecution. Many may now embrace the witch identity for political or spiritual reasons, but thousands of women have suffered and died because of their perceived association with witchcraft.

For centuries, the word "witch" has been used to punish women and to police female sexuality. Now, "slut" has become the damning epithet that is de rigueur. The names and punishments may have changed, but many of the same oppressive attitudes and behaviors toward women that were prevalent during the early modern witch hunts persist. By examining the misogyny that drove the witch hunts, we can illuminate the brutal origins of the sexism women still face today, and put into context feminist resistance against contemporary misogyny. As a new wave of feminism floods both IRL and URL spaces to campaign for women's rights, exploring alternative avenues for liberation often goes hand in hand with exploring alternative philosophies and spirituality. While engaging in the movement for gender equality, more and more millennial feminists are engaging in ritual, trying out tarot, studying herbalism, and following the primordial cycles of the waxing and waning moon. Witchcraft practices that might once have spelled death for women are now life-affirming.

Still, misogyny, misinformation, and myth pervade the legacy of the witch.

So who, exactly, is the witch?

Most of us have a distinct image that comes to mind when our mouths tighten and release to form the word, "witch."

The witch is a shapeshifter. She transforms from vixen to hag, healer to hellion, adversary to advocate based on who seeks her.

She's Hecate, the ancient Greek goddess of the crossroads.

She's Lilith, the blood-drinking demoness of Jewish mythology who refused to submit sexually to her husband.

She's Baba Yaga, the Slavic hag in a chicken-legged hut who flourishes in the forest.

She's Yamauba, the monstrous Japanese mountain crone who feasts on human flesh in her tattered kimono.

She's Joan of Arc, the French military hero in white armor burned by her brethren for cross dressing and heresy.

She's Marie Laveau, the powerful Voodoo Queen of nineteenth-century New Orleans.

She's Elvira, vamping with a crucifix in her bountiful cleavage, dishing out double entendres.

She's Malala Yousafzai, the Pakistani teen shot for her feminist advocacy and awarded the Nobel Peace Prize.

She's the bruja at the botánica.

She's the practitioner of granny magic, hoodoo, and conjure.

She's the everyday intuitive, seeing and hearing things others do not.

She's everywoman.

The witch is at once female divinity, female ferocity, and female transgression. She is all and she is one. The witch has as many moods and as many faces as the moon.

Most of all, she is misunderstood.

From the spiteful old hag to the promiscuous young woman to the man-hating shrew, the negative stereotypes about the women we call witches, sluts, and feminists have filled volumes. Clearing away the cobwebs of connotation is no easy feat, but is vital for a prolonged analysis of these terms.

For the purposes of this book, **feminism** is, as author and social activist bell hooks defines it, "a movement to end sexism, sexist exploitation, and oppression." hooks intentionally does not name men as the root cause of this oppression, but rather gender stereotypes and sexist narratives—which can be propagated by a person of any gender.

The same sexist narratives that suggest a woman's worth lies in her sexual desirability suggest a man's worth lies in his strength—and disregards those who identify outside the gender binary altogether. Culturally entrenched beliefs like these dictate the characteristics one must embody or face the threat of marginalization and violence. In other words, the sexist system is rigged against us all—although women and those on the feminine spectrum have suffered disproportionately because of it.

This sexist system has created the atmosphere for pejorative definitions of "witch" and "slut" to thrive.

Slut is a derogatory term for a sexually promiscuous woman. In its earliest usage in fifteenth-century Old English, "slut" referred to a dirty, slovenly, unkempt woman or maid. By the nineteenth century, it had come to refer to a woman of low or loose moral character. Today, it defines a woman by her perceived or actual sexual activity. Given the pervasive fiction that determines a woman's value based upon her sexual purity, this word has destructive potential.

Although words like "player" or the delightfully old-school "cad" can define a man by his perceived or actual sexual activity, they are most often bestowed as a badge of honor. There are far fewer cultural and religious restrictions placed upon male sexual expression, so such terms are unable to punish men in the same ways their female equivalents can. The core difference in connotation between "slut" and "player" exposes the sexual double standard, where men are rewarded for their sexual activity, while women are punished for theirs.

Witch, like slut, is difficult to define, and yet we all have some understanding of what it means. Similar to Justice Potter Stewart's famous proclamation on pornography, you know it when you see it. (Pardon the parallel.)

The roots of the word "witch" can be found in the Old English words "wicca" and "wicce," which referred to a male sorcerer and female sorcerer, respectively. In Middle English, these words morphed into the genderless "wicche," and by the sixteenth century, our contemporary spelling of "witch" was in wide circulation.

To trace the witch's lineage beyond words, it is useful to uncover how mainstream culture defines her today. Here are four common ways in which "witch" circulates in society:

The first definition reflects how the witch was characterized during the witch-hunting era: the witch is an evil, malicious sorceress (or sorcerer) who is driven by the Devil to do harm.

The second definition follows this line of thinking into vivid aesthetic expressions. The witch embodies the horror of the aging woman: the hag. Female fecundity dried up and worthless to the man looking for nubile flesh and a repository for his seed. Women are frightening for being unattractive, sexually unappealing, and past their prime, and yet, they are frightening when young and attractive because the witch is also charming, bewitching, beguiling, and sexually irresistible with her mysterious feminine wiles.

The third definition brings us into the twentieth century with the Wiccan religious movement. Popularized by Gerald Gardner in 1950s Great Britain, Wicca is a nature-based practice with adherents who often proudly bear the title of "witch." Wiccans are also Pagans, a group of diverse nature-worshippers who number over one million in the United States.

The fourth and final definition of "witch" refers to mathematics. For the curious, the "witch of Agnesi" is a mathematical curve supposedly named after a mistranslation of a 1748 treatise by Italian mathematician Maria Gaetana Agnesi. The term "versiera," meaning "turning," was mistakenly read as "avversiera," a nickname for the Devil's wife, and translated as "witch." Is it a mere coincidence that a male professor at Cambridge translating a female academic's work in 1801 made this mistake?

These definitions can help gauge historical and popular perceptions, but it's imperative that equal weight be given to those who self-identify as witches when discussing this contested word.

To Bri Luna, who founded and runs the popular site The Hoodwitch—a community offering "everyday magic for the modern mystic"—being a witch means: "The power to boldly and unapologetically embrace nature, heal yourself, and heal your community. To respect the seen and unseen realms. It means the freedom to be your most authentic self. To embrace ALL aspects of whoever that may be, and fiercely."

To Wiccan priestess, author, and journalist Margot Adler, "The Witch is woman as martyr; she is persecuted by the ignorant; she is the woman who lives outside society and outside society's definitions of woman."

To "official witch of Salem" Laurie Cabot, the witch

"personifies a woman's ability to intuit, create, enchant, protect, initiate, nurture, teach, and heal."

To artist, curator, and teacher of magical practice Pam Grossman, a witch is "the shadow cast by every woman you've ever known."

As with being a feminist, there are multiple ways to be a witch or to identify with the witch.

Some take part in a spiritual or occult practice with a group—or fly solo.

Some are inspired by the witch as an archetype and eschew the ritual and spiritual altogether.

Many view the witch as the embodiment of a powerful femininity rooted in the earth, which transcends patriarchal influence. Her story begins thousands of years ago.

WITCH SLUT ARE YOU? THE MEDIEVAL TO THE MODERN

The witch has an illustrious, multi-cultural heritage that stretches back to the dawn of civilization. You can find the legacy of the witch in Sumerian tales of Inanna, in Egyptian legends of Isis, and in Hindu myths of Kali. The wonders and horrors of womankind were embodied by these generative, destructive mother goddesses who symbolized both birth and death, light and dark.

"The mysteries of female biology dominated human religious and artistic thought, as well as social organization, for at least the first 200,000 years of human life on earth," write Monica Sjoo and Barbara Mor in *The Great Cosmic Mother: Rediscovering the Religion of the Earth*. And yet, somewhere in the midst of monotheism's dawn, when belief was consolidated around a single male deity, women began to take on increasingly sinister roles in religious and artistic lore.

In Christianity, the witch's earliest ancestor is Eve. The original bad girl of the Bible, Eve is cast as weak and susceptible to Satan, ravenous for forbidden knowledge proffered in apple form by his slithery minion. Eve's actions caused humankind to be cast out of paradise and sentenced to suffer for eternity, and from this origin story, a virulent strain of sexism began to solidify. Prevailing archetypes of womanhood in the Bible become virgin, obedient wife or deviant whore. "Thou shalt not suffer a witch to live," states Exodus 22:18, a directive flanked by advice on how to buy a bride and why you shouldn't commit bestiality.

21

As cultural historian Riane Eisler theorizes in *The Chalice and the Blade: Our History, Our Future*, "If we read the Bible as normative social literature, the absence of the Goddess is the single most important statement about the kind of social order that the men who over many centuries wrote and rewrote this religious document strove to establish and uphold."

When Christianity began to take root in Europe during the first millennium, conflict began to brew between newly minted devotees and those steeped in goddess-worshipping, nature-based faiths. At the time, many people still dedicated themselves to Diana, Roman goddess of the hunt, the moon, and childbirth; and Hecate, Greek goddess of the moon, the crossroads, and witchcraft. According to historian John Demos, many also looked toward folk healers, often called "cunning folk," to engage in practices that would aid love, sex, prosperity, and fertility, using spells, remedies, "fortune-telling, conjuring and countless other practices so humble and obscure they left no traceable record."

These wise women and men would become part of the narrative of witchcraft. However, it wasn't until the Black Plague had wiped out over a third of Europe and Christianity had been molded around a sharp duality between God and the Devil that the stage was properly set for the witch's debut.

By the early modern era, the archetypal witch embodied the fear of female flesh unchained. Devious and obscene, everything about her flew in the face of patriarchal authority. Although Christians did believe in male witches and many men were accused of witchcraft, to discuss witches and witch persecution without addressing the woman-as-witch mythos would be to ignore a robust canon of art, literature, and scripture that conflates femininity with devilry.

"The history of witchcraft is primarily a history of women," explains Carol F. Karlsen in *The Devil in the Shape of a Woman: Witchcraft in Colonial New England*.

To study this history is to peer into the abyss of fear, sexist violence, and toxic masculinity that dominates feminist discourse today.

"All witchcraft comes from carnal lust, which is, in women, insatiable."
—*The Malleus Maleficarum*, 1486

Life in the fifteenth century was far from easy. Most folks were hard pressed to explain the widespread death, disease, and daily hardships they faced, and evil was the simplest scapegoat. Add this propensity for superstition on the part of the Catholic Church to local governments hungry to suppress dissent and assert their dominance, and you have a recipe for conflict.

When the printing press was invented in the mid-1400s, religious propaganda about heathen servants of Satan began to replicate like a viral meme. In these dastardly texts, witches were blamed for a host of everyday maladies and misfortunes, from infant mortality and illness to poor crops and infertility. There was no occurrence too large or too small to attribute to sorcery.

One tome in particular, *The Malleus Maleficarum*, rose above the rest as an exemplary repository of anti-witch sentiments, and catapulted the female sorceress to fearful new heights. It held a treasure trove of quotable quotes, and its chief author, a German Catholic friar and inquisitor named Heinrich Kramer, remains one of witch hunting's most notorious trolls.

Men of the cloth were supposed to be celibate for life, and Kramer knew his audience. What better way to spice up a text about heresy than to make it sexy? *The Malleus Maleficarum* inspired countless cruel deaths, but was also pretty much ye olde medieval BDSM erotica.

It was an entertaining—perhaps even one-handed read— and it's likely certain elite readers at the time thought so, too. Barely a few chapters past the introduction, this diabolical book first published in 1486 covers such burning questions as "the method in which witches copulate with Incubus devils," "whether the act is always accompanied by the injection of semen," and "whether witches may work some prestidigitatory illusion so that the male organ appears to be entirely removed and separate from the body."

There's also a fantastical description of witches stealing penises and keeping them as pets in a bird's nest with other lonely, disembodied penises that crawl amongst each other and feast on a diet of corn and oats. (You can't make this stuff up.)

Despite being disavowed by the Catholic Church in 1490, *The Malleus Maleficarum* "marks a change in Church attitudes," art historian Jane Schuyler explains. In the early medieval era, witches were viewed as mostly benign, "seen as isolated misfits with weird ways that could aid or harm," she writes. Witches of the Renaissance, however, "were held to be heretics in league with the Devil, opposed to the rule of God on earth; they were seductive and immoral, and received their powers as gifts from Satan."

They were also most likely women. This new breed of witch reflected "a pulling together of misogynous attitudes from many different sources and centuries," notes John Demos. And once rumors about their wicked ways began to spread, all hell broke loose.

Sudden tragedies and inexplicable occurrences were cause for suspicion, and a minor interpersonal quarrel or a wayward temperament could spark an inquisition into maleficium. When a woman couldn't conceive? Witchcraft. When a surly old widow uttered an unkind word? Witchcraft. When a young woman refused the advances of a man? Witchcraft.

With little recourse, mothers, sisters, and daughters were accused of witchcraft by husbands, family members, neighbors, local officials, kings, and the clergy. These women were aged widows, middle-aged women, teenagers, and misfits of all classes. At times, men would bear the brunt of witchcraft accusations—but it was often older, poor women who paid the price. A disproportionate number of accused witches were over forty years of age, which coincides with waning fertility, the criterion by which a woman's worth was measured in early modern society.

Although some places were barely touched by the savage campaign against witches, Germany, France, Poland, Hungary,

The Netherlands, Scandinavia, and the British Isles all succumbed to varying degrees. Laws and lore varied from region to region, so procedures differed, but the fear of witchcraft was endemic.

"We know now that witchcraft beliefs were not a monolith of concretized superstitions inherited from the Middle Ages but an evolving bundle of ideas, often with unresolved internal contradictions," clarifies Linda C. Hults in *The Witch As Muse: Art, Gender, and Power in Early Modern Europe.*

Both the Catholic and newly minted Protestant authorities as well as secular government officials were involved in witchcraft trials, but it was the civil courts that would execute the most people. The witch-as-wicked-woman trope may have gotten its start in the church, but the state ran with it, and witchcraft morphed from heresy to treason—a crime against the community itself.

As witchcraft was usually considered a *crimen exceptum,*[*] the trials and treatment of suspects were rarely by the book. Confessions were crucial to such cases, as the crimes were impossible to witness. After a suspect was arrested, she would usually be stripped naked and probed for any tell-tale markings that might betray her alliance with the Devil: a mole, an extra nipple, a birthmark. Then, she would be forced to endure all manner of torture, from whipping, compressing, and stretching to psychological tactics like solitary confinement and lengthy, aggressive interrogations. If she had a fortune or a family, both would be threatened. Christian women were indoctrinated with narratives about the lurking evils of womanhood from their youth, so it stands to reason they could succumb to the belief that they, too, were the Devil's handmaidens—particularly if they had ever committed a sin of any kind. Given this level of torment, it's a wonder everyone didn't crack under pressure and own up to committing nefarious acts at Satan's behest.

"Few witches failed to provide at least some confessional

---

[*] *Crimen exceptum*: an exceptional crime prosecuted outside legal convention.

material that came from experience and drew on the details of daily life," confirms Lyndal Roper in *Witch Craze: Terror and Fantasy in Baroque Germany*. This could be anything from the way the Devil's love gun felt during unholy intercourse (cold and hard) to what the witches' sabbaths were like (killer parties, basically).

Most confessions walked a fine line between pleasure and horror, as both "Catholics and Protestants were convinced that pleasurable sensory experience could be deeply sinful," Roper continues. But whatever admissions of "guilt" were eventually produced can hardly be trusted. The process was corrupt to the core.

Ironically, it was largely because of the witch trials that a woman's testimony would come to be admissible. Up until that time, women were considered dependents of their husbands or male family members and were mostly ignored by European courts.

Anne Barstow details in *Witchcraze: A New History of the European Witch Hunts* how little the legal system paid attention to women until they began to be accused of witchcraft in the mid-sixteenth century. "That European women first emerged into full legal adulthood *as witches*, that they were first accorded independent legal status in order to be prosecuted for witchcraft, indicates both their vulnerability and the level of antifeminism in modern European society," she writes.

Certain types of women—adulteresses, fornicators, and midwives—were singled out as exponentially more evil in *The Malleus Maleficarum*, but it's unclear how often they were put to death in comparison to other victims. Some accounts of the era suggest mostly cunning folk, midwives, or healers were targeted. Others offer alternative explanations.

The writers of the women's health treatise *Witches, Midwives, and Nurses: A History of Women Healers* say, "It's impossible for scholars to offer statistically firm generalizations about the occupation of women accused of witchcraft: usually, the convicted person's occupation was not recorded."

The number of accused witches executed by the church and state also remains unclear. Some feminist writers have put forth reckonings in the millions. In the past few decades, other historians have recalibrated those figures, including Roper, who places the estimate at more than fifty thousand people executed between the late fifteenth and eighteenth centuries—75-80 percent of whom were women.

Barstow explains how difficult it is to settle on a number of "witch" executions. "Working with the statistics of witchcraft is like working with quicksand," she writes, citing destroyed and incomplete records, as well as the unknown numbers of those who died in jail, were murdered after they were acquitted, or committed suicide due to witchcraft stigma. Her estimate is two hundred thousand people accused of witchcraft and one hundred thousand put to death—85 percent of whom were women.

We'll never know the exact number. But quibbling over statistics can obscure the focal point—women were predominantly targeted and female sexuality was centered as a culprit.

"The themes of the witch trials recur with monotonous regularity across Western Europe, featuring sex with the Devil, harm to women in childbed, and threats to fertility," Roper writes, "all issues which touch centrally on women's experience."

"I will slaughter every single spoiled, stuck-up, blond slut . . . those girls I've desired so much. They have all rejected me and looked down on me as an inferior man."
—Elliot Rodger, Isla Vista Shooter, 2014

Women remain demonized in the third millennium.

In America, they are persecuted in the public and private spheres by individual men and entire bodies of male legislators. They are targets for sexual assault, sexual harassment, and laws limiting reproductive rights and abortion access. They are targets of Planned Parenthood gunmen and misogynistic extremists like Isla Vista shooter Elliot Rodger, the twenty-two-year-old who killed six and injured fourteen people in 2014 as vicious payback for his perceived sexual failings. And when women aren't being physically attacked, they are publicly shamed—particularly those who campaign for sexual freedom and reproductive rights.

Witch, meet slut.

In 2012, Georgetown University student Sandra Fluke was called a "slut" and a "prostitute" by conservative talk radio host Rush Limbaugh for testifying at a Congressional meeting on birth control in favor of contraception access.

"If we are going to pay for your contraceptives, and thus pay for you to have sex, we want something for it, and I'll tell you what it is," he announced to his listeners. "We want you to post the videos online so we can all watch."

High-profile women are similarly besieged. Model, entrepreneur, and activist Amber Rose has faced threats, mockery, and stigmatization from strangers and famous exes alike because of her vocal pride in being a former stripper who identifies as a "Certified Slut."

A uniquely twenty-first-century slut-witch hunt is well under way. But inquiring minds want to know: what does it take to earn the hallowed title of "slut"?

As with being called a witch in the Renaissance era, logic and reason have little to do with it.

To be a slut doesn't require being a sex worker, a nude selfie-taker, or a promiscuous woman. Jessica Valenti, author of *Full Frontal Feminism: A Young Woman's Guide to Why Feminism Matters,* sums up the definition of the "s-word" in the title of an article she wrote for *The Guardian* called "What makes a slut? The only rule, it seems, is being female."

Although any woman can be deemed a slut, more explicit erotic actions are an express ticket to the top of the list. And contrary to what some might think, slut-shaming (aka being judged for your real or perceived sexual expression) isn't solely perpetrated by men.

A 2014 study by a cross-party think tank found that women on Twitter slut-shame other women almost as much as men do. A 2013 study by Cornell University published in the *Journal of Social and Personal Relationships* found that female participants rated a hypothetical woman with twenty sexual partners "as less competent, emotionally stable, warm, and dominant" than a hypothetical woman who had only had two.

This same-sex prejudice was alive and well during the witch-hunting era, when women frequently accused other women of witchcraft.

"Women—and other oppressed groups—sometimes try to outdo their oppressors in scorning persons perceived as outsiders, in hope of being accepted, or tolerated, themselves," writes Anne Barstow in *Witchcraze*. "In the witchcraft trials, the poor attacked those even poorer; marginalized women attacked those women even further out of power than they."

Even Amber Rose admits to being a former slut-shamer.

"I used to call women sluts and whores all the time," she told *The Guardian*. "Because that's what society taught me: that that was OK and that it was what I was supposed to be doing. . . . But I grew up, and I have seen these issues, and I have become very passionate about it. I am a former slut-shamer and a newfound feminist."

To combat the contemporary epidemic of slut-shaming, victim-blaming, and sexual assault, Rose has hosted multiple SlutWalks in Los Angeles. Originating in 2011 in Toronto, the SlutWalk movement was inspired by one police officer's comment that women could avoid harassment and assault if they stopped "dressing like sluts." Since then, SlutWalks have been held all over the world, from Rio de Janeiro to New Delhi, with varied success in highlighting issues of race, class, gender identity, and sexual orientation within the discourse on sexual assault.

As a queer woman of color who grew up poor, Amber Rose's involvement with the SlutWalk has arguably helped to deflect its designation away from that of a straight, middle-class white woman's movement. Whatever critiques have been leveled at the SlutWalk, however, its global impact in challenging rape culture is undeniable.

Named by feminists in the 1970s, rape culture is the pernicious discourse that normalizes violence against women through everything from jokes, advertisements, and films to national laws and criminal procedures. Rape culture is teaching women how to avoid rape instead of teaching men not to rape. It's the song that glamorizes coercive sex. It's the narrative that says most reports of sexual assault are false. It's the light sentence given to a young male rapist because the judge believes he has a promising future. It's the rape joke and the audience that laughs along.

The editors of *Transforming a Rape Culture* describe rape culture as "a society where violence is seen as sexy and sexuality as violent . . . [and] women perceive a continuum of threatened violence that ranges from sexual remarks to sexual touching to rape itself. A rape culture condones physical and emotional terrorism against women as the *norm.*"

During the witch trials, physical and emotional terrorism against women was indeed the norm. Although sexism was expressed differently in the early modern era, destructive male hegemony motivated by religious, political, and economic interests remains largely intact today. As the initial parallels between the witch and the slut reveal, slut-shaming and rape culture are poisonous blooms from the seeds of misogyny sown centuries ago. When Europeans began to cross the Atlantic, they brought this legacy of brutality to American soil, where it would take root in disturbing new ways.

ALL-AMERICAN WITCH: SALEM'S LEGACY

The restless townspeople crowd together in the courtroom, scowling uneasily at the two accused witches who sit opposite the judge. They jeer and murmur, the women alternately shouting and goading their husbands to confess what sorcery they've seen. In a skit depicting 1692 Salem, comedians Amy Schumer and Bridget Everett are on trial for wreaking havoc on the town's men.

Infusing history with her brand of brash humor, Schumer's 2015 "Wingwoman" episode from Season 3 of *Inside Amy Schumer* tackles the Salem witch trials by riffing on the deep-seated anxieties about women and female sexuality that have inspired countless accusations of witchcraft around the world.

"They're not women. They are witches!" one woman in the courtroom shouts, and by her husband's sheepish admission, the two plainly dressed Puritan "witches" caused strange physical symptoms in the menfolk, from bruises on their necks to, as another man puts it, "a fiery pain in my shaft upon evacuation" and "a harrowing rash of redness down there."

It's hard not to titter at descriptions of these New World STIs.

After a few more men testify, we soon find out that these witches' powers do indeed come from below—well, below the belt. Schumer and Everett's "black magic" lies in their "shorn mounds," reveals one exasperated man, and anyone who dares glance into the tavern of their employ is likely to be drawn in by their wicked ways.

The judge, played by a bewigged Colin Quinn, has heard enough. Pounding his gavel on the podium to regain order, he announces the verdict.

With eyes downcast and hair askew, the two cowering "witches" are deemed guilty of bewitching the townspeople and sentenced to burn at the stake. They shudder painfully at their fate before shuffling over to plead with the judge. After a few moments of whispering inaudible (sexual) favors into his ear, Quinn overturns their punishment following their presumed offer to overturn him. He orders everyone out, immediately, so they can seal the deal.

As the angry mob filters toward the door, one man stops to inhale the scent of the bench where the two witches just sat. His wife, alarmed, chastises him.

"What?" he shrugs, exasperated, "I'm under a spell!"

If tragedy + time = comedy, then the writers of *Inside Amy Schumer* have capitalized on the zeitgeist to not-so-subtly lay out the links between witch hunting and slut-shaming as they bubble to the surface.

Although the sketch is light on historical facts—there were no witch burnings in Salem, and the women put on trial were not known sex workers—it cuts to the core ideology behind many witch persecutions: a belief in the inherent wickedness of women.

Like the witches on trial in Schumer's Salem, women remain on trial in the court of public opinion. Are her fictional "witches" blamed for inciting male lust and sparking community strife any different from the women blamed for inciting their own rapes, the sex workers blamed for the violence committed against them, or the young girls forced to adhere to different dress codes lest they inspire dangerous desires in their male classmates? Throughout history, female sexuality has been held responsible for both society's men and their morality.

Ask anyone educated in America about Salem, and they're likely to come up with a salacious tidbit about that eventful year. It's nearly impossible to escape middle school history without learning something of the Satanic panic unleashed in the small New England village. Dozens exhibited strange symptoms and hundreds were implicated in inflicting a witching on unsuspecting members of their community.

Although the European witch hunts saw thousands of deaths and aren't commonly included in American history textbooks, Salem saw fewer than fifty deaths, yet most students learn something about the Salem trials in school. This is arguably due to a dash of American cultural myopia, the phenomenon's allegorical function, and the draw of popular art and literature spun from Salem's legacy.

I surveyed fifty Americans of diverse ages and backgrounds in an informal Q&A on Salem, and though everyone was familiar with the brouhaha, misinformation abounded.

Some claimed hundreds were put to death (fourteen women, five men, and two dogs were executed), while others believed the guilty were burned at the stake or drowned. (They were all publicly hanged in front of friends, family, and community—save for one man, who was pressed to death.)

In addition, many respondents confused the terms "Puritan" and "pilgrim."

"Puritan" was initially a derisive term used to refer to English Reformed Protestants in the sixteenth and seventeenth centuries who set out to "purify" the Church of England of its Catholic influence. They were persecuted in England, which drove many to seek haven in America. Today, the word is most associated with prudery, something of which the Puritans were also enamored.

"Pilgrim" is the word for any traveler on their way to a holy place. Consequently, many Puritans were also pilgrims on their way to a promising New World.

The final—and more erroneous—misconception I encountered? That Salem was the largest witch hunt ever. As you read in the second chapter, that is not true by any stretch of the imagination.

This uniquely American witch hunt straddles both history and mystery, and despite a bounty of studies on the subject, there is no single explanation as to what stirred the pot in Salem village—although historians have their theories.

Pulitzer Prize–winning author Stacy Schiff collected a list of causes in her 2015 book *The Witches: Suspicion, Betrayal, and Hysteria in 1692 Salem*. She writes: "Our first true-crime story has been attributed to generational, sexual, economic, ecclesiastical, and class tensions; regional hostilities imported from England; food poisoning; a hothouse religion in a cold climate; teenage hysteria; fraud, taxes, conspiracy; political instability; trauma induced by Indian attacks; and to witchcraft itself."

Whichever of these you believe, the Salem witch trials arguably took up where the European witch trials left off and featured a familiar confluence of circumstances.

The living conditions in seventeenth-century America, like those in Europe, were harsh. In the Northeast, brutal winters coupled with the threat of invasion by local tribes and inter-community conflicts laid the foundation for paranoia, and prevailing Puritan doctrine only heightened the fear that evil lurked behind every corner. The differentiating factor in the Salem trials, however, was the cadre of young women who set the turmoil in motion.

Sometime in the frigid winter of 1691–2, two prepubescent girls in Reverend Samuel Parris' household began acting strangely, taken with frothing fits and tormented by unseen evil. They howled and contorted, sometimes appearing deaf, dumb, or blind. They were pinched and pricked by invisible agents and could not be left alone. After no physical illness could be ascertained, it was determined the Reverend's daughter and niece, Elizabeth Parris and Abigail Williams, were suffering from something psychic. The girls were eventually diagnosed as bewitched by a local doctor.

Soon, Betty and Abigail's strange symptoms were exhibited by other young women in Salem village. At a time when proper deportment for Puritan girls included speaking infrequently and quietly, and with deference to male relatives, such recalcitrant behavior caused quite an uproar. When doctors, parents, and religious authorities compelled the growing group of girls to reveal the origin of their maladies, Sarah Good, Sarah Osborne, and Tituba Indian were named as those responsible.

They were three outsiders: Good was a surly beggar, Osborne was a widow embroiled in local disputes, and Tituba was a slave from Barbados owned by Reverend Parris. Warrants were issued for their arrest, and they were brought in for examination in late February of 1692.

Questioned first, Good denied all claims of hurting the girls, but soon diverted the blame to Sarah Osborne.

Good's husband, when put on the spot, said she was an "enemy to all good," and if her wickedness hadn't yet devolved into witchcraft, it would eventually. Their marriage was clearly on the rocks.

Osborne, up next, denied Good's accusation, but did conveniently mention a dream she had starring a black spirit that pinched her and dragged her by the hair.

Next to be interrogated was Tituba, who cut to the chase and admitted she was forced into Satan's service by Good and Osborne and other "witches" in Salem village. Her confession was gilded with descriptions of hirsute beasts, flying via broomstick through the night sky, and signing the "Devil's book," where she spotted the signatures of Good and Osborne, among others.

Tituba described the Devil as a tall man with white hair dressed in black clothes, a description that some historians— including Katherine Howe in *The Penguin Book of Witches*—say aptly fits Tituba's master, Samuel Parris. It isn't a stretch to guess he served as a tormenting dark lord to her on earth.

As the number of bewitched girls increased, the witch hunting fervor spread.

Carol F. Karlsen theorizes that in New England's Puritan culture, severe restrictions on thought and behavior could cause fits, seizures, and bouts of breathlessness. For the young women at the center of the trials, their possessed behavior offered release.

"As the community looked on, their bodies expressed what they otherwise could not: that the enormous pressures put upon them to accept a religiously based, male-centered social order was more than they could bear," Karlsen writes.

To wheedle out the witches, the authorities began to use some of the young afflicted girls as witch finders, giving them status far above their birthright. According to Schiff, this could have something to do with "why we have turned a story of women in peril into one about perilous women."

Months wore on, and sister blamed sister, husbands blamed wives, and neighbor accused neighbor. There was no affliction or occurrence too extreme or benign to pass off as the devious workings of a witch. Everything from rancid butter to spectral evidence of an accused witch's apparition causing mischief around town served as proof of witchcraft. Some accused witches were quick to confess, offering details of their workings to avoid the gallows. They admitted to Satanic baptisms, sorcery carried out via poppets or divining boards, and enchanting animals, friends, and family members. Many were spared, but others were not so lucky.

By 1693, nearly two hundred people had been accused of witchcraft, more than fifty had confessed, nineteen had been executed, and a few perished after months of languishing in jail.

By 1706, more than a dozen people involved in the trials—from judges and jurors to accusers—would publicly state their regret over getting swept up in the mania and sending innocents to their death.

☿

Female bodies and minds were envisioned as dark, noxious spaces inclined to vice in seventeenth-century New England. Women were the weaker, more corruptible sex, and their perceived link with the Devil was strong. As occurred in the European witch hunts, women of all ages and backgrounds were accused in Salem, but the majority executed were over forty, and the men accused and executed were often related to accused female witches. Forced confessions, torture, and strip searches for the Devil's mark or extra teats for an animal familiar to suckle all made an appearance, along with revelations of the witches' sabbath, riding on broomstick, and signing the Devil's book.

And yet, the Puritans were relatively chaste in their witch dealings when compared to their European counterparts. Stacy Schiff reveals that New England witches "rarely enjoyed sexual congress with the Devil." Granted, female sexuality has never been viewed fondly by patriarchal figures unless they are penetrating its warm embrace, but it did not play as large a role in Salem or in other American witch hunts.

The American witch trials weren't nearly as bawdy as Amy Schumer's comically exaggerated skit might suggest. No, our Puritan "ancestors" were apparently too prudish to imagine the ways witches could be as slutty as those across the pond. Whereas carnal bacchanals were freely depicted in art and scripture during the European witch hunts, the American witch hunts were far more buttoned up.

This repressive view of sexuality, female sexuality in particular, is still infused into American politics—and the American psyche.

THE MIDWIFE: BESTIAL BODIES & REPRODUCTIVE RIGHTS

Dressed in rags or pristine linen, her skin was likely ruddy from decades of soaking in the elements. Cold and matter-of-fact or uncompromisingly warm, she dispensed potions to cure aches and pains, to expedite labor, and to prevent pregnancy. She knew the machinations of the body only whispered about outside polite company. She was privy to the screams behind the door: the spitting horrors of childbirth, the secrets of sexual congress. In an era when men knew even less than they do today about women's internal affairs, the midwife held power that stretched past her gender and station.

During the witch-hunting era, the female figure most intimately acquainted with sex, birth, and fertility was the midwife. Armed with knowledge of herbology, biology, and, in particular, reproductive health, these predominantly poor, peasant women were easy targets for accusations of sorcery.

"No one harms the Catholic Faith more than do midwives," proclaimed *The Malleus Maleficarum*, with an explanation for such vitriol summed up in a chapter titled "That in Various Ways Midwife Sorceresses Kill the Fetuses in the Womb and Cause Miscarriages, And When They Do Not Do This, They Offer the New Borns to Demons."

Because they dealt with the mysterious, liminal space between birth and death, sickness and health—and specialized in the needs of women—midwives were viewed as suspect not only by the church and state, but also by patients and their families. Before the scientific method was widely accepted, midwives relied on time-tested natural remedies (in addition to spells and charms) including painkillers, anti-inflammatories, and digestive aids, many of which remain in use today.

Barbara Ehrenreich and Deirdre English explain in *Witches, Midwives & Nurses* that when an ailment treated by a midwife didn't heal, witchcraft could be to blame, and yet, if an ailment was healed, witchcraft, too, could be to blame. "There was no problem in distinguishing God's cures from the Devil's, for obviously the Lord would work through priests and doctors and not through peasant women," they write. This was, after all, an era "when the Church held that pain in labor was the Lord's just punishments for Eve's original sin," Ehrenreich and English continue.

Witchcraft was frequently associated with sex-related crimes. Midwives and women who were discovered teaching birth control methods or providing abortifacients or abortions were often also accused of witchcraft. Driven by a fear of infanticide and abortion, the 1556 French Parliament ordered pregnant women to register their pregnancies and required a witness for their deliveries. If they did not do so and their baby died, they would be subject to the death penalty.

Although midwives were, no doubt, accused of witchcraft, the extent to which they were is contested by contemporary scholars. But whether midwives were a majority or a minority of women tried and executed does not change the fact that their profession was looked down upon by religious and medical authorities.

Historians also debate how much the denigration of midwives was based in a real fear of their supposed black magic capabilities or if it was merely a smokescreen for acute gender bias. Hilary Bourdillon suggests in *Women as Healers: A History of Women and Medicine* that "it was not so much the type of healing being practiced by the wise-woman which laid her open to the accusations of witchcraft, but the fact that she was an unlicensed healer." Midwives could be seen to receive their healing powers from the Devil, but they could also be seen as circumventing the male-dominated medico-religious system.

Witch hunting continued throughout the Renaissance era, and midwifery became progressively licensed and regulated by the state. Women still consulted midwives for abortions, contraception, and fertility issues, and midwives still came into conflict with the medical establishment—particularly during the New England witchcraft cases. "The frequency with which doctors were involved in witchcraft cases suggests that one of the unspoken (and probably unacknowledged) functions of New England witchcraft was to discredit women's medical knowledge in favor of their male competitors," explains Carol F. Karlsen.

By the mid to late 1800s, witch hunting had all but ceased, but the campaign against midwives continued in subtler forms. *When Abortion Was a Crime: Women, Medicine, and Law in the United States, 1867–1973* author Leslie J. Reagan notes that the early anti-abortion movement was partially an effort by the American Medical Association to discredit midwives and establish the primacy of "real" (male) doctors.

Although the execution of midwives and female healers would come to be viewed as a grievous error of the past, many men—often in positions of power—remain willfully ignorant of biological facts regarding sexual and reproductive health. Religious and government officials leveraging their positions to thwart female bodily autonomy is still very much an American reality.

In 2012, Republican Senator from Pennsylvania Rick Santorum weighed in on the subject of contraception, echoing a sentiment one might find during the witch trials. Birth control is "not okay," he said. It's a "license to do things in the sexual realm that is counter to how things are supposed to be."

That same year, Republican Congressman from Missouri Todd Akin explained in a TV interview that pregnancy doesn't occur from rape, so there need not be a special legal abortion exemption for such cases. "If it's a legitimate rape, the female body has ways to try to shut that whole thing down," Akin said, igniting a firestorm of feminist pushback against this patently false statement.

In 2015, Idaho State Representative Vito Barbieri followed his fellow Republicans in voicing another confoundingly uneducated comment. During the testimony of a medical doctor, Barbieri revealed his lack of anatomical knowledge, asking if a camera could be swallowed and end up inside the uterus to check out "the situation" down there.

Also in 2015, non-profit women's healthcare provider Planned Parenthood was accused of illegally selling tissue from aborted fetuses for profit. Led by anti-abortion activists, this Republican-driven campaign was labeled a "witch hunt" by women's health advocates. At the time, Texas Governor Rick Perry described the (now disproven) allegations of tissue profiteering "a disturbing reminder of the organization's penchant for profiting off the tragedy of a destroyed human life."

Planned Parenthood provides prenatal care, pap smears, breast cancer screenings, STD testing, and sexual education to millions of underserved women and their families. Despite the fact that the Hyde Amendment has prohibited funding for almost all abortions since 1976 and that abortions do not nearly make up the majority of Planned Parenthood's services, Congress voted to federally defund the healthcare provider. When the bill was vetoed by President Barack Obama, he said: "Because of the harm this bill would cause to the health and financial security of millions of Americans, it has earned my veto." This executive action was but one small triumph in an ongoing onslaught of attempts to limit women's healthcare access.

During the 2016 election season, Republican nominee Donald Trump furthered his party's trend of anti-woman attitudes, saying there should be "some form of punishment" for women who seek abortions—before backpedaling hours later. His running mate Indiana Governor Mike Pence (who believes condoms offer "very poor protection against sexually transmitted diseases"), later announced that he wanted to see Roe v. Wade "consigned to the ash heap of history where it belongs."

It remains to be seen just how far the Trump/Pence administration will roll back reproductive freedoms.

The early modern witch hunts served in part to discipline and punish female bodies. According to Silvia Federici in *Caliban and the Witch: Women, the Body and Primitive Accumulation*, the witch hunts can be also linked to "the contemporary development of a new sexual division of labor, confining women to reproductive work." This sexual division of labor largely remains intact, and the women who seek to undermine its supremacy by exerting control over their own reproductive function are often viewed through the same lens accused witches once were. Today's "sluts" seeking birth control and basic reproductive freedoms are hardly different from Satanic witch midwives of yesteryear.

Misinformation and demonization have been consistent threads in the history of women's sexual and reproductive health. A majority of Europeans and Americans may no longer believe women's bodies are likely to be bewitched by the Devil, but "the curse" is still slang for menstruation. The church and state may no longer exterminate midwives, but the lingering stereotype of midwifery as filled with duplicitous shrews persists. The phrase "old wives' tale" echoes some of this cultural bias, as there is no equivalently gendered term for a man who delivers supposedly harmful, naïve, and unscientific advice. These attitudes and turns of phrase may seem innocuous, but are vestiges of a barbarous history.

Despite immense social and scientific advances over the past six centuries, politics, religion, and women's health remain inextricably entwined. Like the inquisitors, witch finders, and civilian accusers of yore, Republican lawmakers and their ongoing attacks against sexual and reproductive health place a woman's right to bodily autonomy perpetually under siege.

POLITICAL WITCH: REBELLION & REVOLUTION

"For rebellion is as the sin of witchcraft"
—I Samuel 15:23

"The woman who possesses love for her sex, for the world, for truth, justice and right, will not hesitate to place herself upon record as opposed to falsehood, no matter under what guise of age or holiness it appears."
—Matilda Joslyn Gage, *Woman, Church and State*

"Witches have always been women who dared to be: groovy, courageous, aggressive, intelligent, nonconformist, explorative, curious, independent, sexually liberated, revolutionary."
—W.I.T.C.H.

Cloaked in black, a faux pregnant belly, and a crown of thorns, the national spokesperson for The Satanic Temple, Jex Blackmore, shouldered a large, wooden cross in front of a Detroit Planned Parenthood clinic on Good Friday. Unnerved members of the Pro-Life Action League looked on. Two men and a woman with the names of anti-abortion Michigan representatives scrawled onto their jackets followed Blackmore, unfurling their leather floggers on her with a crack. The expectant mother strode forward with her cumbersome cross, symbolic assailants in tow. She walked past protesters with signs that read "We are praying for your baby" and "Don't do this to your baby."

On March 25th, 2016, Blackmore, a Satanist, feminist, and witch, staged this arresting tableau with her comrades to highlight the very real persecution of women by a doctrine that elevates embryos above all else.

The term "Satanic" is highly fraught. It strikes fear into the hearts of many believers who see Satan as the embodiment of evil. Like the word "witch," it has frequently been used to vilify women and invoke scenes of sinful fornicators.

Formed in the new millennium, The Satanic Temple is a nontheistic organization dedicated to Satanic practice and the promotion of Satanic rights. They view Satan as the "Eternal Rebel against arbitrary authority," but do not worship Satan as a deity. Instead, TST uses its status as a religion to enact political change and "to encourage benevolence and empathy among all people, reject tyrannical authority, advocate practical common sense, and promote justice." Over the past few years, they have worked tirelessly for feminist issues such as reproductive rights, LGBTQ rights, and the separation of church and state.

Like many of TST's protests steeped in guerrilla theater, the Good Friday "Sanctions of the Cross" procession detailed above was "a testament to the burden of oppressive mandates endured by women who are forced to consider the religious opinions of the legislature while making personal family planning decisions."

The names singled out on the backs of the floggers are significant because they are the names of the men and women in power abusing the separation of church and state to create laws with a Christian agenda.

"Just as the church commemorates the flagellation of Jesus by the Roman soldiers, the Temple acknowledges the role played by Michigan Senators and Representatives in keeping women under the church's law," TST stated. Little explanation is needed, however, when you see this darkly stylish scene.

As an artist, activist, director of the Detroit chapter, and national spokesperson for TST, Jex Blackmore has made headlines organizing visceral and visual protests, and for documenting her own abortion process through the Unmother Project. Inspired by aesthetic activism that originated in the 1960s with groups like the Yippies and W.I.T.C.H., Blackmore's work harnesses the power of the diabolic woman for revolutionary means.

In early 2016, Blackmore and TST publicly claimed the witch a potent symbol of rebellion. Before the release of Robert Eggers' *The Witch*, Blackmore declared that the horror film "departs from the victim narrative" of witchcraft and stands as a "declaration of feminine independence." To raise awareness about The Satanic Temple's activism and how the puritanical witch hysteria depicted in *The Witch* parallels the contemporary political climate, TST held four interactive, multi-media "Sabbat Cycle" events across the country.

"Nearly four-hundred years after the first execution of an American 'witch,' many in our nation still call for the establishment of an American theocracy and a return to the puritanical delusions of old," reads the Sabbat Cycle mission statement. "In the face of relentless persecution, of unjust authority treading on our private, intellectual and sexual lives, we, the outsiders, the freethinking, and the godless have found ourselves strengthened."

The Satanic Temple's national, four-part series marked a new visibility for the witch as a political icon. It was hardly the witch's first foray into politics, however. To understand the witch's transformation from a servant of Satan to an engine of activism—and back again—requires a look at the early days of the feminist movement, when women were first seeking a figure emblematic of their struggle.

☿

Picture this: Glinda the Good Witch, in her spangled crown and frothy, pink tulle gown. She welcomes Dorothy when the Kansas ingénue shows up in Oz, wide-eyed and frightened. She wields her glittering star-tipped wand with grace, each movement rustling her puffy sleeves and voluminous petticoats. She is motherly and soft-spoken, embodying classic feminine qualities.

"Are you a good witch or a bad witch?" she asks Dorothy, glancing down at Toto. Parroting back a stereotype that originated in the European witch trials, Dorothy replies that she cannot be a witch because "witches are old and ugly." The Munchkins laugh off camera, because little does Dorothy know.

Inspired by an early feminist and foremother of women's suffrage, Glinda is one of the first explicitly "good" witches to be depicted in popular media—first in L. Frank Baum's 1900 book, *The Wonderful Wizard of Oz*, and later in the 1939 MGM film adaptation, *The Wizard of Oz*.

Although her green-faced twisted sister might be more memorable, there are a lot more layers to Glinda than you'd think.

Don't underestimate our most iconic femme witch just because she's pretty in pink.

Even those with a cursory knowledge of feminism are familiar with the nineteenth-century "suffragettes."* We know their stern, proper countenances from the pages of grade school textbooks. We know that many began in the anti-slavery movement as abolitionists and were then inspired to begin advocating for women's rights.

But what we don't often learn is just how witchy they were.

Elizabeth Cady Stanton was a key organizer of the Seneca Falls Convention in 1848, the first convention on the rights of

---

* Originally, "suffragette" was coined as a term of derision for suffragists, but some women's voting rights advocates reclaimed the term and wore it with pride.

women. Stanton composed the "Declaration of Sentiments"—a feminist manifesto signed by one hundred men and women at Seneca Falls—at a table normally used for séances.

In *Other Powers: The Age of Suffrage, Spiritualism, and the Scandalous Victoria Woodhull*, Barbara Goldsmith reveals that

Stanton was a practitioner of Spiritualism (and that suffragist **Susan B. Anthony** was a fan, too). The popular nineteenth-century belief system centered around communing with the dead via séances conducted by mediums, who were often women bestowed with status and respect because of their intuitive abilities. "Miraculously, the ideas began to flow" once Stanton put pen to paper on the hallowed spot, and her blow to gender inequality was crafted with inspiration from beyond.

Known for her passionate oratory skills, **Sojourner Truth** was born into slavery but escaped to become a renowned abolitionist and women's rights activist. Despite not being able to read or write, she published an account of her life to sell so she could support herself, and once won a $125 award from a libel case against a newspaper that published a story calling her a witch. Although Truth did not take kindly to that term at the time, historian Nell Irvin Painter argues that Truth's syncretic spiritual practice, which blended West African animistic beliefs, American folk magic, and Dutch Calvinism and Methodism does makes her a witch in the contemporary sense of the word.

Truth's impassioned "Ain't I a Woman" speech at the Ohio Women's Convention in 1851 vocalized the painful realities of racism and sexism that she experienced throughout her life. Long before the dawn of intersectional feminism, Sojourner Truth declared that the fight for women's rights must take women of color into account.

Victoria Woodhull was a free love and reproductive rights advocate who once made her living as a psychic and Spiritualist medium. In 1872 she also became the first woman to run for president of the United States, running on a ticket that included abolitionist leader Frederick Douglass as her vice president.

A sex worker and equal opportunity slut, Woodhull is said to have saucily proclaimed: "I am a very promiscuous free lover. I want the love of you all, promiscuously. It makes no difference who or what you are, old or young, black or white, pagan, Jew, or Christian, I want to love you all and be loved by you all, and I mean to have your love." Her legacy is carried on today by the Woodhull Freedom Foundation, which works to "affirm sexual freedom as a fundamental human right."

Matilda Joslyn Gage embraced a reclamation of the divine feminine as her spiritual practice, and is the first known suffragist to reclaim the word "witch." An abolitionist who purportedly offered up her home as part of the Underground Railroad, Gage was also a dedicated campaigner for women's rights. In 1893, she wrote *Woman, Church and State*, a searing indictment of patriarchal religion and the collusion of church and state. Well over a century later, her anti-clerical book barely seems dated, and stands as a witch-infused rallying cry for gender justice.

In its pages, Gage discusses Christian misogyny as it relates to the European witch trials and humanizes the persecuted witch, while providing inspiration for L. Frank Baum's characterization of Glinda in *The Wonderful Wizard of Oz*. As Baum's mother-in-law, the elder stateswoman of feminism had a major impact on his writing, says Matilda Joslyn Gage Foundation founding director Dr. Sally Roesch Wagner. Without Gage, witches might still be viewed as solely evil in popular culture.

Before reclaiming language and stigmatized figures was deemed a viable political tool, Gage was reassessing the legacy of the witch, actively working to challenge conceptions of the witch's role in history. In Gage's estimation, witches were not maleficent sorceresses, but women targeted by the Christian state. She theorizes that the word "witch" "formerly signified a woman of superior knowledge," and her analysis of the witch trials is in line with that of many contemporary feminist historians:

> In looking at the history of witchcraft we see three striking points for consideration:
> First: That women were chiefly accused.
> Second: That men believing in women's inherent wickedness, and understanding neither the mental

nor the physical peculiarities of her being, ascribed all her idiosyncrasies to witchcraft.

Third: That the clergy inculcated the idea that woman was in league with the Devil, and that strong intellect, remarkable beauty, or unusual sickness were in themselves proof of this league.

As radical feminist Mary Daly rhapsodizes in the 1980 introduction to a reprint of Gage's book: "Gage's method is not merely chronological but Crone-logical." (See what she did there?)

Daly continues: "The madness in her method will appeal to every witch who reads the work (and for 'witches,' as Gage suggests, we can read 'women,' in order to gain fuller comprehension of the cruelties inflicted by the church upon women)."

The idea of every woman as witch—and as political dissident—has its roots in Gage's work.

By the feminist explosion of the 1960s, the time was ripe for the witch to be revived and regaled as a political symbol, and the Women's International Terrorist Conspiracy from Hell were just the women for the job.

> "If you are a woman, and dare to look within yourself, you are a Witch."
>
> —W.I.T.C.H.

In late 1968, the conflict in Vietnam was raging, Martin Luther King had been assassinated, and the women's liberation movement was diversifying and splintering into a variety of political action groups. One of these was New York City's W.I.T.C.H.

Approximately thirteen women created this confrontational coven on Halloween in 1968, including feminist luminaries Robin Morgan, Florika, and Naomi Jaffe. As Alice Echols explains in *Daring to Be Bad: Radical Feminism in America 1967–1975*, they were inspired by the Yippies (Young International Party), who were known for "organizing through outrageous acts."

W.I.T.C.H. took guerrilla theater to the next level, drawing on fears of the wicked woman by fashioning themselves in her image. Dressed in Halloween-chic shifts and pointy black hats, and brandishing broomsticks with comedic flair, W.I.T.C.H. members set their sights on capitalism and corporations as the engines driving sexism of the day. Soon, chapters materialized in Washington, D.C., Chicago, San Francisco, and other big cities, and the W.I.T.C.H. acronym was repurposed for each unique action a group would undertake (Women Interested in Toppling Consumption Holidays, for example).

Some W.I.T.C.H.es would hex the New York Stock Exchange or don black veils to protest a bridal fair while chanting "Here come the slaves, off to their graves." Others would fight back against office sexism at a telephone company, interrupt a Senate hearing on population control, or mail nail clippings and hair to a university that fired a radical feminist professor. Draped in black, W.I.T.C.H. took to the streets, chanting with hands clasped, summoning their collective power to make a scene and mobilize.

Like many activist organizations, W.I.T.C.H. was not without a dash of youthful naïveté. As co-founder Robin Morgan notes in *Going Too Far: The Personal Chronicle of a Feminist*, those involved had not "raised our own consciousness very far out of our combat boots."

But whatever they may have lacked in ideological clarity and maturity, they made up for in audacity and shrewd sloganeering.

This heady brew of Macbethian protest language W.I.T.C.H. crafted for the "Conspiracy Against Women" chant could easily be revived today by your own activist coven:

Double, bubble, war and rubble,
When you mess with women, you'll be in trouble.
We're convicted of murder if abortion is planned.
Convicted of shame if we don't have a man,
Convicted of conspiracy if we fight for our rights.
And burned at the stake when we stand up to fight.

By donning witch drag, W.I.T.C.H. lent the weight of history and mythology to their activism, and pushed witches into the national spotlight once more. Throughout the 1960s and 1970s, the witch's prevalence in pop culture and politics would solidify her as a martyr mascot for the women's movement. Writer Nora Ephron even invoked the witch in a 1972 article for *Esquire* when she analyzed the growing fractures within feminist leadership: "Betty [Friedan] as Wicked Witch of the West, Gloria [Steinem] as Ozma, Glinda, Dorothy, take your pick," she wrote.

Although the original W.I.T.C.H. covens may have been short lived, their tradition survives in the twenty-first century, both in new activist covens around the country and in figures like The Satanic Temple's Jex Blackmore, who is radically reconceiving political protest.

In a 2016 talk that *Slutist* sponsored as part of the Legacy of the Witch festival, Blackmore described her brand of Satanic feminist activism to a rapt audience at Catland Books in Brooklyn. She emphasized how women are demonized today, particularly in the battle for reproductive rights, and she challenged the historical association of Satanism with masculinity.

"The Satanic Temple represents an evolution in Satanic philosophy, which aims to dismantle archaic sexual paradigms and give voice to those who have suffered under the yoke of Satanism as a pejorative," she said.

Prior to her talk, I sat down with Blackmore over libations to discuss her politics and process.

How did you come to Satanism personally and politically?
I self-identified as a Satanist after I left the church because I felt like the church I belonged to in my teenage years was oppressive to my human nature. I also found the way that the church described sinners and people who were immoral was just like how I was. I feel like I am much more aligned with a Satanic figure. Being part of the punk and metal subculture, I was particularly frustrated in how apathetic and insular it was. To be apathetic and indifferent to me is so contrary to alternative or

punk ideology because you're giving in to those who seek to oppress you.

The Satanic ideology has always been one of rebellion. So, we as Satanists should be engaged in political activism. When TST announced their existence and I met up with them, we discovered our ideas were very much aligned and so we started working together. That was three years ago now, around 2013. It's incredible to think about how much has happened in that short amount of time.

Let's talk about what you call your "aesthetics of resistance." So much political action is denigrated when there's a visual element, particularly when it's feminist political action, with groups like Femen or the SlutWalk. Why is it so important to have an aesthetic? What does it add that other movements, which don't have an aesthetic, lose?
We live in a very visual culture with the internet and marketing and everything being packaged to look a specific way. With attention spans shrinking, you kind of have to aestheticize your work to touch on a cultural pulse that people respond to. I can see other movements that lack that feature, and I feel like they could be much more successful if they would employ a powerful aesthetic. Young people specifically are drawn to that.

You don't have to release a huge, complicated statement if you have a powerful visual element as a communicator. Essentially you have to figure out the way you can best communicate with people, and I think art and aesthetic are the most powerful tools we have to translate complex issues.

Who are your biggest influences for guerrilla theater and why?
I'm a big fan of Abbie Hoffman and the Yippies, the Women's Action Coalition, and W.I.T.C.H. When you feel like you don't have a voice, and don't have power, often your only choice is to employ radical means as a way to create power where there is none. It's social currency. If I go talk to a legislator, they're not going to listen to me. I don't have the power and resources to get

hundreds of thousands of signatures for a ballot issue. Sometimes political theater is one of our best tools.

What other groups have harnessed the occult or the witch in their activism like W.I.T.C.H. did?
The Yippies tried to levitate the Pentagon. No one else has really aligned themselves with the occult like W.I.T.C.H. did, and I think part of it is that it's hard to do, it's dangerous, and it works against you as much as it is empowering.

What connections do you see between witches and feminism?
The idea of the witch has always been about subversive feminine power that doesn't align with conventional norms. It has been used to control and demonize women consistently: women who had privileged economic positions, women who were smart, women who had expertise in medicine, women who were outspoken, women who were sexually promiscuous. Female independence and sexual independence is still frightening because it liberates us from oppressive structures and having to rely on a patriarchal system to grant us power.

HILLARY CLINTON: WICKED WITCH OF THE LEFT

In 2016, the witch archetype was brandished with new fervor in the presidential election. Hillary Clinton, the Democratic presidential nominee, former Secretary of State, Senator from New York, and First Lady of the United States was the witch to be immolated.

When "bitch" won't suffice to denigrate a woman, "witch" adds an element of supernatural evil that has no male equivalent in common use. Public, powerful, and controversial women from Congresswoman Nancy Pelosi to conservative commentator Ann Coulter have been branded with the term—although none more frequently than Hillary Clinton.

A target because of her gender, her personality, and her policies, Clinton has been defamed with the word "witch" for decades. A brief online image search for "Hillary Clinton + witch" or a scroll through the #WitchHillary hashtag will offer a multitude of memes and cartoons featuring the stateswoman consorting with Satan or depicted with green skin and cackling, melting, or flying high—often in full Wicked Witch of the West regalia.

During the 2016 campaign, Republican nominee Donald Trump, his campaign surrogates, and his supporters called Clinton "Crooked Hillary." She was a "bitch," a "tramp," and the "Wicked Witch of the Left" connected with "Lucifer"; she deserved to be lynched, locked up in chains, or executed in a firing line, they said. She was "Hildabeast Clinton," a "nasty woman" out to destroy humanity with her "Vagenda of Manocide." But in one of the most heated election seasons in decades, it was not only Republicans who vilified her.

Chanting in support of Democratic Socialist presidential candidate and Senator from Vermont Bernie Sanders in early 2016, some devotees transformed his campaign slogan "Feel the Bern" to "Bern the Witch" at rallies. One man even took it upon himself to create a "Bern the Witch" fundraiser on Sanders' official website, which was eventually removed and criticized by the Sanders campaign after it was highlighted by an advocate for Clinton.

Trump's campaign only stoked anti-Clinton sentiment amongst their supporters, however.

"Give her a broom so she can fly away, that witch," said Trump crony and actor Antonio Sabàto Jr. in an interview on Fox News.

"She's a witch with a capital B," declared Rush Limbaugh on his radio show.

The commentary kept on coming, and after a virulent display of Clinton-hate during the Republican National Convention, the Hillary-as-witch rhetoric reached a boiling point. Even Clinton's camp felt the need to comment, and sent out a pointed email on the subject. Titled "a witch hunt," the message from Christina Reynolds, Deputy Communications Director of Hillary for America, was simple. Drawing comparisons between the witch trials of old and the demonization of her candidate, Reynolds wrote:

I thought the behavior at the RNC couldn't get a whole lot worse. Tuesday night proved me wrong.

Chris Christie, the governor of New Jersey . . . stood on stage and accused Hillary of being a criminal, bellowing "GUILTY" over and over again as the crowd egged him on.

He had the entire arena chanting "lock her up"—a cry that has become the mantra of the RNC.

*If you closed your eyes, you could imagine it being
a lot like a witch trial—they were barely one step removed from screaming "burn her at the stake."*

John Demos explains in *The Enemy Within* that the witch
hunt as metaphor is "a mode (most often) of moral reproach."
You'll find the label readily affixed when there appears to be
"some allegation of subversive intent, of conspiratorial menace,
of concealed betrayal."

The phrase has most often been used to damn a genderless party, corporation, or group, whether it be the GOP's witch
hunt against Planned Parenthood, or the liberal media's witch
hunt against basically anyone in the GOP. In 2016, however,
as Donald Trump, his advisors, and supporters declared Hillary Rodham Clinton a criminal in league with evil—and one
who should be bound in chains and executed—the brutal gendered dimension of the historical witch hunts was reanimated
in frightening new ways. And it only got worse as the election
season wore on.

In August, Trump referred to what might happen if Clinton
were to win the presidency. Nothing could stop her from nomi-
nating liberal Supreme Court justices, he told a crowd in North
Carolina, except "Second Amendment people—maybe, I don't
know." Many Republicans, Democrats, and journalists heard his
statement as a call to arms for gun owners to take matters into
their own hands and assassinate her, despite Trump's disavowal
of this interpretation.

During the second presidential debate, Trump threw yet
another verbal dagger, elevating Clinton's position within the
medieval demonological pantheon from witch to "the Devil,"
referencing Bernie Sanders having made a deal to support her.
At the time, Trump was newly embroiled in controversy after a
salacious 2005 tape from *Access Hollywood* was released. It revealed him boasting to host Billy Bush that "when you're a star,"
women let you do anything you want to them. You can even

"grab them by the pussy," he bragged, cavalierly suggesting he had engaged in sexual assaults.

Demonstrating just how high America's tolerance for sexism had become, Trump soon regained a foothold in the polls, dismissing his previous comments as "locker room talk." The Republican candidate who made a public habit of rating women by their desirability, denigrating women's physical appearances, and slandering any woman who dared challenge him didn't stop there. Trump made another public, sexist jab at Clinton in the third and final debate during a moment of juvenile smugness, interrupting Clinton dismissively to call her a "nasty woman."

It would be an understatement to say that misogyny ran utterly unchecked in Donald Trump's 2016 presidential campaign. The heinous rhetoric that Trump and his surrogates employed to damn Clinton in apocalyptic language arguably baited the Christian right by stirring up biblical fears of witches and wicked women. Many Clinton supporters, however, celebrated these terms of derision, subverting them proudly in solidarity. After Clinton clinched her nomination for president at the Democratic National Convention, *Salon* published an article putting a new spin on her witchiness, titled "Kudos to Hillary for playing the woman card: If people are going to call her a witch, she'll tell them she's Hermione Granger."

Writer Amanda Marcotte name-dropped J.K. Rowling's most studious, level-headed witch in the title, drawing parallels between the *Harry Potter* character and Clinton's leadership style.

She then took issue with the kind of denigration Clinton has faced, writing, "The claims that her haters make about her—that she's mendacious, manipulative, bossy, and shrill—bear no relationship to the woman herself, but sure do sound exactly like the same things people have always said about women who seek power and independence, since the days such women were burned as witches."

More editorials positioning Hillary Clinton as a shrewd sorceress were published as Halloween drew near. Coincidentally, a new conspiracy theory arose at the time, which suggested Clinton participated in a cannibalistic "spirit cooking dinner" at performance artist Marina Abramović's house, in addition to more claims that she was legitimately part of a Satanic witch's cult.

The reviled-woman-as-witch discourse grew to a fever pitch during the final months of the campaign. As Trump supporters swore in dead seriousness that Hillary was in league with the Prince of Darkness, Clinton supporters wore "Hags for Hillary" and "Witches for Hillary" buttons and rallied around the idea of the first witch in the White House. They declared themselves #NastyWomen with a #Vagenda for equality, ready to destroy Trump in the voting booth and #GrabHimByTheBallot.

Despite these valiant efforts, Clinton managed to secure a decisive win with the popular vote—receiving nearly 2.9 million more votes—but Trump dominated in the electoral college, winning the bid to be president in 2017. Sexism was not the sole reason Clinton lost the presidency, but the waves of misogyny that pummeled America throughout 2016 undoubtedly played a major part in it.

"On Tuesday November 8, the country proved its misogyny runs deeper than most of us could have ever imagined," wrote Jessica Samakow in the *Huffington Post*. "We chose to elect a man who has admitted to sexual assault over the most qualified candidate in history, who happens to be a woman."

"We, as a culture, do not take women seriously on a profound level. We do not believe women. We do not trust women. We do not like women," wrote Lindy West in a piece expressing her disgust with the election's outcome in *The New York Times*.

In the most misogynistic election season to date, people on both sides of the political spectrum consistently invoked the witch. As both the apotheosis of evil femininity and an emblem of female strength in the face of oppression, the witch once again played the role she is best suited to play—the shapeshifter. Whether the witch appears a horrible, Satanic hag or a knowledgeable, capable woman has everything to do with who calls her into being. She always reflects the beliefs of her beholder.

☽♀☾

The day after Donald Trump's inauguration, women—and witches—gathered in protest. In marches across America and around the world, millions showed up for women's rights and social justice. Sign after sign alluding to witches and witchcraft were spotted by witch-identified activists and shared on social media. "We are the daughters of the witches you failed to burn," announced one. "Brujas against racism, sexism, ableism, transphobia, homophobia, and billionaires with shitty grammar," proclaimed another.

A new W.I.T.C.H. coven in Portland marched in head-to-toe black, faces covered in opaque veils to maintain anonymity as they carried signs painted with "Witches For Black Lives," "Trans Women Are Women," and "Thou Shalt Not Suffer The Patriarchy To Live." In Denver, the triple goddess symbol adorned a placard reading "You can try but you cunt divide the tribe." In New York City, "Witches Against Trump" made an appearance, and in San Francisco, "Hex The Patriarchy" was on display.

The prevalence of witch-infused messaging at this historic moment in support of gender equality reaffirmed the witch's continued role in feminist activism. She stands strong as a wellspring of resistance against patriarchal abuses of power, and unity in the face of bigotry. A "witch" may not be in the White House, but witches are still in the streets.

ART WITCH: WANTON WOODCUTS & DOMESTIC GODDESSES

Grinding lasciviously on phallic staffs, cavorting nude with horned beasts, and whispering unholy incantations into the blackened sky, the witch was depicted as progressively lurid in the early Renaissance.

After *The Malleus Maleficarum* stoked the public's desire for demonic raunch, the first illustrated witchcraft treatise, published in 1489 by German legal scholar Ulrich Molitor, finally put a face to this Satan-loving sorceress. "On Witches and Female Soothsayers" features woodcut prints of witches embracing the Devil, half-human, and half-animal creatures riding cooking forks, witches gathering around a cauldron, and witches gabbing with their wicked sisters over a meal.

"I think we take it for granted now in our copy-paste culture that everything is so easily replicable and meme-able," explains curator, teacher of magical practice, and author of *What Is a Witch* Pam Grossman. "Molitor's treatise is like the earliest meme of what a witch looks like."

According to scholar Natalie Kwan, more editions of Molitor's treatise would be printed between 1489 and 1669 than even *The Malleus Maleficarum* itself, which begs the question which text had a greater impact on how Europeans saw the witch. Molitor's work would also go on to infiltrate fine art, influencing heavyweights such as Hans Baldung Grien, Albrecht Dürer, and untold others.

"You have hundreds of years of art history where men, at least on record, were the ones creating images of witches," Grossman says. "Sometimes they were really sexy, young temptresses that would lead to your downfall, and sometimes they were hags who literally boiled babies and cast hexes on you."

To wit: Hans Baldung Grien's 1515 woodcut "Standing Witch with Monster" shows a young, voluptuous sorceress in the midst of an unholy 69 with a dragon-like creature as she plumbs its orifice with a rod and appears to excrete fluid from her nether regions into its mouth. There is a toddler on the monster's head, sticking its fingers dangerously close to its teeth, and a baby lying near the curl of its tail.

Francesco Maria Guazzo's 1608 woodcut "The Obscene Kiss" features a witch poised to bury her face between Satan's buttocks—a greeting thought to solidify the bond between witches and their dark lord.*

Luis Ricardo Falero's 1878 painting "Witches Going to Their Sabbath" envisions a swirling torrent of nude witches, bats, and winged demons—some mounted on broomsticks, some mounted on each other—on their way to a saturnalian soirée.

Since the early modern era, most depictions of the witch—and of women in general—have reflected male subjectivity and have catered to male desire.

In *Ways of Seeing*, art critic John Berger details how nudes in Renaissance art are portrayed as sexual objects to be viewed by a presumed male spectator outside the painting. Although "the principal protagonist is never painted," Berger writes, his specter looms large. "It is for him that the figures have assumed their nudity. But he, by definition, is a stranger—with his clothes still on."

The prurient images of nude witches described above reflect this dynamic, as well as the creative dominion of men in the field of image making. According to Linda C. Hults' analysis of the witch in visual art, paintings of witches by the likes of

---

* The Latin term for Satanic analingus is "osculum infame."

Dürer and Baldung no doubt "fostered misogyny, often directly by engaging the debate about the reality of and the appropriate judicial and social response to witchcraft." At the same time, they subtly invoked "early modern ideas of artistic creativity as an exclusively male realm," she explains.

As more female artists began to craft their own visions of magical women, however, the witch finally began to transcend the well-worn binary of nubile temptress or vile hag. By the late nineteenth century, the witch had become more than just a sight for the eyes of men, acquiring her own subjectivity, and in turn, her humanity.

I spoke with Pam Grossman about this transformation, and how female artists remade the witch in their own image, changing how the public saw her in the process.

What cultural factors were at play to change depictions of the witch in art?
I see the parallel rise of the Spiritualist movement and the Theosophical religious movement to be the driving factors in how magical women were re-pictured in art.

In the mid-nineteenth century you have the growing popularization of cameras, and at the same time you have Civil War widows who are grieving and desperate to contact their lost loves—and so spirit photography is born. You have séances and the Spiritualist movement which was largely led by women who believed they could contact the dead, and this planted a lot of the seeds for the suffragette movement. Victoria Woodhull, the first woman who ran for president, was also a medium. So for the first time, women are the religious leaders, women are the direct connection between the earthly realm and the heavenly realm, and they believe they have this divine power.

In 1875, Madame Blavatsky starts her Theosophical Society, which posits that all religions have some truth to them, and that if you pull back the veil of symbols and context there's this greater holy truth that unifies us all.

So you have her, and a lot of artists like Kandinsky and

Mondrian who are inspired by her. And this idea of the artist as being a channel for spirit begins to take firmer hold.

You also have the occult revival happening in Europe, including the start of the Hermetic Order of the Golden Dawn, which, unlike Freemasonry, had female members on equal footing with the men. Suddenly you have women who have power and voice in these spiritual communities. These women are seekers, writers, scholars, and a lot of them are great orators and artists as well. And hand in hand with their male collaborators, they start to create art about their experiences.

Who were the first female artists to depict the witch and take back her representation?
Decades later you have the female surrealists who are interested in the occult. They are inspired by all of these prior occult movements. They are also weaving together threads from different esoteric systems of study like Kabbalah and tarot and the I-Ching and their own autobiographical imagery, and putting all of this into their paintings.

When you think about Remedios Varo, Leonora Carrington, Leonor Fini—I think Frida Kahlo to some extent, although I don't necessarily see her as part of the same lineage—their work is very autobiographical and infuses the domestic female sphere with magic and mythology. If you look at their paintings, you see kitchens, you see the domicile, you see their pets. Images of ritual and metamorphosis are happening within their own houses. So suddenly the home is depicted as this magical cauldron space.

By inserting themselves—and femaleness in general—into their visual stories, these women are staking claim and taking control of the narrative about the magical woman archetype. They're identifying with her as artists, and reclaiming the role of "witch" as a positive one both in their work and in their lives.

So the witch is no longer a horrible, depraved creature who will lead to your downfall. Because of these artists, we are shown that there are parallels between witchcraft, womanhood, and art, the connecting factor being creativity. We see that whether one is doing ritual, engaging in magical practice, cooking, studying, painting, writing, sculpting—it's all holy work.

How do you see that practice continuing in the twentieth and twenty-first centuries with the witch in feminist art?
This through line continues with feminist art in the 1960s and '70s, which I actually see as having a lot of parallels with the Surrealists in several ways—trying to re-sacralize the female experience. Even though "female arts and crafts" take just as much skill as painting or drawing, for thousands of years they were traditionally considered to have less value than the work done by male artists. Sewing and ceramics and working with textiles—this is all incredibly laborious work, despite having domestic roots. So it was feminist artists who fought to elevate these mediums to the institutional level, and deem them worthy of attention and investment.

And a lot of the feminist artists would have references, whether blatantly or not, to the divine feminine or witchcraft in their work. Judy Chicago is a great example of this. Her work is deeply political and about many, many things such as gender and society and commerce, but she also mentions magic specifically in some of her pieces. Most famously, she created "The Dinner Party," which is essentially a giant shrine to the divine feminine and feminist history that you can visit in the Brooklyn Museum. It's a glossy, black room with a table in the shape of a triangle with thirteen place-settings at each side to honor female deities and important women throughout history. It uses iconography that is obviously very vaginal, with erotic floral plates and iridescent chalices. This to me is one of the most witchly art pieces that has ever been created.

What's occurring now, with the fourth wave of feminism crashing, is that many female artists are using occult images, ritual gestures, and witch iconography to not only connect to the divine, but to continue to make space for themselves in a field which is still dominated by men. They're utilizing herbs, candles, ceremonial garb, and goddess imagery, and mashing it up with digital treatments and modern technology. As such, they're turning themselves into witches: women who create things and shift perception, who trust their intuition, and who have the power to change the world. Their work is spiritual and political at the same time.

GHOST BITCH U.S.A.

Three men in Puritan garb hold down a girl in white. In front of an American flag, their hands rummage inside her gaping body cavity while a beer bong is shoved down her throat by a man wearing a Boston Red Sox cap. He pours two bottles of booze into her mouth as her eyes remain open, wide as saucers. She is petrified and powerless amidst the gang of assailants.

A pilgrim woman in grey wields a veiny, outsize penis. Against a backdrop of American eagles in red and blue, she smashes the member onto a decapitated male pilgrim's head. It spurts semen high into the air with the triumph of retribution. She looks serene and joyful, his gaze lifeless beneath a black buckle hat.

Through powerful, perverse, and political tableaux like these, Rebecca Goyette draws parallels between the persecution of Salem witches and contemporary misogyny. She is not the first contemporary feminist artist to feature the witch in her work, but her connection to America's witch trials is unique. From the hand of direct descendant of hanged Salem "witch" Rebecca Nurse, Goyette's visions serve as sobering historical allegory and biting satire.

For her 2016 "Ghost Bitch U.S.A." exhibition at New York

City's Freight + Volume gallery, Goyette set out to create art that would honor her ancestor Rebecca Nurse and alchemize her own repressed memories of sexual assault as a young girl.

As Goyette created her paintings, drawings, costumes, and hand-crafted items for a Ghost Bitch altar, she found her attention drawn to the 2016 presidential election. Soon, Donald Trump's incendiary, divisive rhetoric became another focus of her art, and she lampooned him through a satirical and witchy castration short and in grotesque paintings and sculptures. The centerpiece of the show, however, was a performance-based video titled "Ghost Bitch: Arise from the Gallows," which stars Goyette playing a historical reenactor by day and dominatrix by night.

As a pilgrim woman, she is hanged violently in a simple grey dress in front of a frothing audience, and as a domme, she dons ethereal white lingerie peppered with extra teats, referencing the Puritan belief that witches had additional nipples strewn all over their bodies for their animal familiars to suckle.

Through psychosexual sequences that include cathartic BDSM scenes starring Boston "bros" barking like dogs, cleansing rituals, and fervid moments of masturbation with silken phalluses, Goyette unveils the lurid absurdity of sexual politics and patriotism in both seventeenth-century Salem and twenty-first century America. In a show that was both timeless and timely, Goyette laid bare the roots of homegrown hate.

I interviewed her the week "Ghost Bitch U.S.A." opened to discuss the genesis of her artwork.

A lot of the work in your show has a feeling of retribution, taking back that power from your ancestor who was powerless. Can you speak to that?
Yes, Rebecca Nurse was left for dead in an unmarked grave, along with her fellow accused witches. Their dead bodies were just piled on top of each other after they were hanged. Along with my breakdown of ancestral violence, my work also expounds upon vibes I was feeling growing up in a male-dominated, racist, small town. I wanted to claim territory not as

a victim but as a person who can truthfully speak about my own experiences.

I am not playing Rebecca Nurse per se in my films. I probably more relate to Bridget Bishop, a bawdy tavern owner and the first one hanged in the Salem witch trials. When I step into character, I play with my own emotional agency through performance. The video camera acts as a mirror, reflecting back to me how I react to different situations, from the near-death foibles of shooting an aerialist hanging scene to sadomasochistic pet play gone awry. Sometimes my characters learn something way before I do, with a fearless push beyond normative boundaries.

Where did the name "Ghost Bitch" come from?
As Ghost Bitch, I'm the ghost of a Puritan, and I chose the name "bitch" instead of "witch" because I'm butting up against this idea of what we call a damnable, wicked woman. As Rush Limbaugh named Hillary Clinton a "witch with a capital B" in her rise to presidential power, we women find ourselves in the throes of public perception looping through the annals of Salem Witch history.

I am not a witch, Rebecca Nurse wasn't a witch, but as Ghost Bitch I haunt; I don't allow for forgetting.

Ghost Bitch spans time. In my video, *Ghost Bitch: Arise from the Gallows*, I play a freelancing witch in Salem who is performing in historical reenactments by day and is working as a dominatrix by night. In the drawings, I think of Ghost Bitch engaged more literally with time travel, compressing and convoluting the present-day timeframe and 1600s Puritan New England.

There's a big critique of American masculinity in your work, whether it's dealing with Donald Trump or male Puritans of years past. It seems part of what this show is saying is that the legacy of Puritanism continues to this day.
Trump just calls up a lot of old baggage in America. People don't realize the roots of American violence, and the fact that they

once would take a woman and put her in jail with seven or eight men inspecting her naked body for extra nipples that her animal familiars would supposedly suckle on. From today's perspective one can only imagine this to be a sexual assault, sanctioned and hidden by the prison system. After lengthy stays in torturous jail cells, the women (and a few accused male witches) were publicly hanged.

When I shot my hanging scene for *Ghost Bitch: Arise from the Gallows*, one of the hanging pilgrims drank an entire bottle of whisky and wanted to put the rope around my neck without my harness on. I refused: the rope was thirty feet long and suspended over a pipe and if that rope got disturbed, it could fall off the pipe, and hang me with the sheer velocity of it falling to the floor. It felt abusive. I argued with him onstage, breaking character for fear of my life. It was a very strange evening collectively because there were actual physical fights that broke out within the diversely populated audience, spurred on by historical anxieties and misogynistic aggression. The film shoot felt like *The Jerry Springer Show*, but not staged, it was very real.

The filming of this first scene of *Ghost Bitch: Arise from the Gallows* was super intense and took a while for me to digest. In the past I was making costumed lobster pornos, and improvising a little lobster sex just doesn't get that crazy. Now, all of a sudden, I was improvising a hanging scene. The fights that broke out onstage and in my studio audience felt like we were reenacting United States history from the hangings of the Salem witch trials to the lynchings of the Jim Crow South. Within the space of an aerial theater, we collectively, psychically relived horrible American nightmares.

It brings to mind the Sandra Bland case, how she was stopped and beaten basically for being a strong black woman. Her arrest, what happened in her jail cell, and the suppression of evidence that ensued are no different in content and context than the groping and assassination of the victims of the Salem witch trials. Bland supposedly hanged herself, but she was taller than the ledge from which she allegedly hanged.

The legacy of lynching started during the witch trials. Certainly I'm not trying to say women are any more or less important, but they were literally some of the first people publicly hanged in America. Puritan men hanged their wives, sisters, mothers, their female landowners, their healers, their sluts, their heretics, their unmarried, outspoken women, their tavern wenches. That tells you something about the kind of society we were establishing as early settlers. We created a public spectacle out of murder during the witch trials, and the United States continued to create a murderous spectacle hanging African Americans during the Jim Crow South era and beyond, to our current media display spreading viral videos of police brutality today.

What art and also earth-based religions can do is to refuse the social control suggested by spectacle-based acts of violence perpetrated by our leaders and in our communities. We have agency through art and ritual to create our own constructs that in turn lead others out of the darkness.

Reflecting on the power of Ghost Bitch as a massive collaborative creative action, I was able to bring together artists, witches, local communities, and audiences to participate in art-making, performing, and ritual in an effort to contemplate our collective American history and to feel it viscerally together. Many Americans and global citizens are seeking a more positive path forward, and artists and new age spiritual practitioners of all sorts can ignite this change. Focusing our collective, creative, humorous, spiritual, and sexual powers against the forces of oppression has been and forever will be the mission of Ghost Bitch U.S.A.

TITUBA'S LEGACY

During the European witch hunts, outsiders and those per-ceived as "other" were always first to be suspected of sorcery. Race did not play a part in most witchcraft accusations, howev-er, save for in Salem.

Addressing issues of racism, oppression, and witchcraft, author Maryse Condé draws conclusions about black wom-anhood and the redemptive nature of ancestral spirituality in *I, Tituba: Black Witch of Salem.* Her ironic, fictional tale rescues the story of Tituba—one of the first three women accused of witchcraft in Salem—from the refuse bin of history.

"Tituba looked for her story in the history of the Salem witch trials and could not find it," renowned activist and scholar Angela Y. Davis writes in the foreword to a reprint of the book. "I have looked for my history in the story of the colonization of this continent and I have found silences, omissions, distortions, and fleeting, enigmatic insinuations."

Condé uses the mock-epic protagonist of Tituba to explore the tensions between witchcraft, feminism, race, gender, and sexuality in American history—and to critique Puritan patriar-chy. Cobbled together with facts and inventive fiction, Tituba's character address many of the myths about the real-life Tituba that have circulated since the witch trials.

Although there are no records of Tituba practicing Voo-doo or teaching the girls of Salem love spells (as Arthur Miller imagines she did in *The Crucible*), in Condé's book Tituba does practice her own brand of syncretic spirituality—an infusion of West African and Caribbean traditions, replete with herbalism and nature-based worship. And although Tituba does not explicitly call herself a witch, she is confused as to why the term would be perceived negatively.

She asks, "Isn't the ability to communicate with the invisible world, to keep constant links with the dead, to care for others and heal, a superior gift of nature that inspires respect, admiration, and gratitude?" She then echoes a question voiced by countless witches, saying: "Shouldn't the witch (if that's what the person who has this gift is to be called) be cherished and revered rather than feared?"

In addition to questioning the ways witchcraft is viewed at the time, Tituba is also confused why the white Puritan women she encounters are so emphatically sex-negative and misandrist.

In the face of her master's wife's prudery, she doubles down on her view of sex as healthy and pleasurable. "For me it's the most beautiful act in the world," Tituba exclaims, while Goodwife Parris responds in horror, "Be quiet! Be quiet! It's Satan's heritage in us."

In the face of her friend and *The Scarlett Letter* alum Hester Prynne's misandry, Tituba responds with open-heartedness to men, despite having been wronged by many of them. When Prynne mentions feminism to Tituba (in an ironic, anachronistic twist), she suggests that Tituba is too fond of sensual pleasures to identify with the philosophy. This can be viewed as both a critique of the misandrous and sex-negative threads within contemporary feminism, and Condé's nod to the ambivalence some women of color have expressed toward a movement initially built to fight for the rights of white women alone.

Although women of color have historically faced increased rates of sexual assault, sexual stigma, police brutality, and poverty, mainstream feminism has not addressed these issues adequately. In 1993, Kimberlé Crenshaw coined what would become third- and fourth-wave feminism's central theory,

intersectionality, to name the racist sexism and sexist racism that women of color encounter.

Crenshaw explained her concept of interlocking forms of oppression as they pertain to domestic violence, writing, "the experiences of women of color are frequently the product of intersecting patterns of racism and sexism. . . . Because of their intersectional identity as both women *and* of color within discourses that are shaped to respond to one *or* the other, women of color are marginalized within both."

Twenty years later in 2013, feminist writer Mikki Kendall created the #SolidarityIsForWhiteWomen hashtag to raise awareness about the lasting racial divides within the feminist community and to give feminists of color a space to contend with gender politics under white supremacy.

She explained in *The Guardian*: "White feminism has argued that gender should trump race since its inception. That rhetoric not only erases the experiences of women of color, but also alienates many from a movement that claims to want equality for all."

By using the tale of America's most notorious black "witch" as a jumping off point, Angela Davis comments upon this complex relationship many black women have with the movement for gender equality.

"Tituba engages in recurring meditations on her relationship—as a black woman—to feminism," she writes, and "her voice can be viewed as the voice of a suppressed black feminist tradition, one that women of African descent are presently reconstituting—in fiction, criticism, history, and popular culture."

In historical accounts of the Salem witch trials, Tituba is an instigator who disappears from official records once she is acquitted and released from jail. In Condé's story, Tituba is a complex, sexually enlightened healer and intuitive. Giving the witch subjectivity is the first step to humanizing her, and the first step to humanizing the countless women who have been accused of practicing witchcraft. Like *The Wonderful Wizard of Oz*, the book *I, Tituba: Black Witch of Salem* is a literary work that has the power to shift popular perceptions about who the witch is. And if the witch is *everywoman*, fighting to liberate the witch from oppressive narratives—be they fact or fiction— means fighting to liberate all women from the same.

TWITCH OF THE TONGUE: LANGUAGE AS SPELL

"'Tis the Whore, that is clamorous"
—Reverend Cotton Mather, *Ornaments for the Daughters of Zion*

"And then our arrows of desire rewrite the speech, mmh, yes."
—Kate Bush, *The Sensual World*

Language is a powerful force.

In Europe and America during the fifteenth through eighteenth centuries, even a whisper of the word "witch" spelled trouble.

It wasn't a term you threw around carelessly.

While witch accusers knew how to wield the word, witches themselves were also thought to use language that would betray their aptitude for wickedness. In many trials, evidence was brought forth of an accused witch muttering something under her breath, saying something strangely, or speaking with erudition beyond her station.

Scholar Jane Kamensky writes about the importance of female speech in New England witchcraft accusations, explaining that "the witch's speech revealed the full destructive potential of the female voice. The witch's cursing, the demoniac's roaring: These were the ultimate ravages of women's words left unchecked."

The "right" kind of woman would never speak thusly.

Famed New England minister Cotton Mather—a notorious supporter of the Salem trials—wrote at length about proper linguistic deportment for proper women in 1692. It was best to hold one's tongue, be soft spoken, and think before you speak. "'Tis the Whore, that is clamorous," Mather declared.

Women's language is similarly policed today. We are told that raising the pitch at the end of our sentences (uptalk) and speaking from the low, creaky spot in our larynx (vocal fry) makes us seem ditsy and immature. We are told that if we say "sorry" too much, it makes us sound weak. We are told that if we use words such as "like" or "um" or "just" (filler words) we are undercutting our intelligence and betraying a lack of confidence in our own ideas.

And yet, female speech can be a space of resistance.

"Witch."

"Slut."

"Feminist."

The ways we speak and the words we say have radical potential.

Used similarly to police and persecute women, "slut" and "witch" make bittersweet bedfellows.

These "darketypes"* are evocative yet nebulous designations and often say more about the person applying these labels than the intended recipient.

Both words encapsulate the stereotypes women are shackled with living in a male-dominated world, but both can also be understood to signal female empowerment. By simultaneously accepting and refuting patriarchal perspectives, some women have come to relish these words with transgressive gusto.

"Slut" is currently caught in the crosshairs of an intra-feminist debate. Some who have suffered from the slings and arrows

---

* Darketype: a dark archetype steeped in shadow with shifting, multivalent meanings.

of this gender-based epithet are taking it back in their own unique ways—but not without pushback from others who feel it's better left unsaid.

Author of *I Am Not a Slut: Slut-Shaming in the Age of the Internet* Leora Tanenbaum has studied the term and its usage for over two decades, and she is an outspoken advocate of obliterating it from our vocabularies. In an interview with *The Guardian* Tanenbaum revealed that some of the girls she interviewed for her books try to repurpose "slut", but end up "losing control of the label when their peers turn it against them"—with some even experiencing sexual assault as a result.

There are also some women of color who contest the ways white women use the word "slut" because of their experiences being cast as promiscuous for merely existing in a racist world. Dr. Carolyn West explains that since the early days of the slave trade in America, the "jezebel" archetype—a racialized version of "slut"—has "branded Black women as sexually promiscuous and immoral" and has been used to "rationalize" a host of atrocities committed against them.

Writer and activist Lutze B. invokes this legacy of misogynoir when discussing her resistance to the term "slut" in *Salon*: "In order for me to claim my right to be a 'slut,' I first must win the battle to be able to fully claim my humanity. . . . As a black woman, I won't be concerned with reclaiming my inner 'slut' until white women show more interest in being in solidarity with me."

Women nevertheless approach this word differently based upon individual and cultural lived experiences. Not all can wear and discard the signifiers of slutdom so easily, but there is no one type of woman who is for or against the reclamation of "slut."

"I fervently hope for the day when we can use 'slut' and 'ho' as a feminist punch line and a badge of honor," Tanenbaum wrote in *The Huffington Post*, "but we aren't there yet. Only when we can be certain that most people agree that women have the right to sexual equality can all women be free to take back these words and make them ours."

And yet, there are many women who associate feminist power with the word "slut." Where some hear vicious misogyny in a single syllable, others hear freedom, sexploration, and self-love.

Sexuality doula Ev'Yan Whitney spreads the slut-positive gospel of Sex, Love, and Liberation through her blog and coaching service of the same name—and embraces the slut identity. After documenting her own struggles with sexual self-acceptance and erotic redemption through deeply personal writing on the subject, Whitney didn't just take her newfound freedom and run, but instead now dedicates her days to midwifing other women through the same process. She defines slut as "a sexually liberated woman, someone who completely owns her erotic self, who loves her sexual body, and gives herself permission to express and actualize her desires however she chooses."

Writer Pilar Reyes believes being a slut means transcending sexual rules. "'Slut' is opening yourself up to the possibility of pleasure and love and touch in myriad incarnations, be it fleeting and drunken, sudden and intense, or slow building and long lasting. Slut is sex for the sake of sex. Pleasure because it feels good. Seeking out lovers and finding your orgasm because, fuck it, you can, so why waste time with all that other bullshit when you can experience the sensation of your skin on someone else's skin instead? Slut is the realization of your sexual freedom and doing whatever the fuck you want with it."

Ritual designer, intuitive, and body worker Emily Tepper says being a slut means "pulling the Patriarchy out of your ass and owning your sexuality without getting arrested or institutionalized."

Artist, queer porn performer and witch Lexi Laphor explains that being a slut means: "Creative expression! Being brave and honest. Loving yourself and others enough to deconstruct desire and find out more about yourself and your lovers! Refusing to be limited or shamed by people who are committed to misunderstanding you."

Feminist burlesque producer and performer Bunny Buxom says slut is synonymous with sexual freedom: "Slut" means "owning, experiencing, expressing, and celebrating one's sexuality."

The act of embracing the term can even be viewed as a philosophy unto itself: "Slutism."

Musician and writer Joshua Strawn coined the term for *Slutist* in 2013, describing the process of reclaiming language as "semiological aikido."

Slutism is "a disposition that embraces its appetite for cultural, intellectual, and physical joys," he explained. "Slutism starts by accepting you can't please all the people all of the time and you shouldn't even try. It requires a nimble literary-mindedness that can interpret context on the fly, in contrast to literal-mindedness."

Slutism is embracing the "mmh yes," as Kate Bush sang, to "rewrite the speech."

Outside of niche communities, "witch" has only come into popular parlance in the past few decades. Before the twenty-first century, it was, similar to "slut," avoided like the plague. Instead, words like "intuitive" or "wise woman" were used as euphemisms for the dreaded "witch." This is one reason why W.I.T.C.H. was able to harness the term for political action in the 1960s so effectively.

As witch, author, and ecofeminist Starhawk writes in her 1979 book *The Spiral Dance: A Rebirth of the Ancient Religion of the Great Goddess,* "to reclaim the word *Witch* is to reclaim our right, as women, to be powerful."

A decade later, Laurie Cabot encouraged every woman to celebrate the word "witch" in *The Witch in Every Woman,* declaring, "the first step to reclaiming your magical nature is to be able to say the word *Witch* aloud, if not to the world at large, then privately to yourself." Cabot describes this magical nature as inner strength, which can also be conceived in nontheistic ways.

There are still witch-adjacent terms like "hag," however, which are slower to catch on. Although many may not use the word "hag" in a positive sense just yet, honoring the prowess of older women is something the words "hag" and "crone" can achieve, at least according to radical feminist philosopher Mary Daly.

In *Gyn/Ecology: The Metaethics of Radical Feminism*, written in 1978, she gives a playful yet persuasive explanation of these two terms, and why their connotation and denotation should be rethought:

"Our foresisters were the Great Hags whom the institutionally powerful but privately impotent patriarchs found too threatening for coexistence, and whom historians erase. Hag is from an Old English word meaning harpy, witch," she explains. "Hag is also defined as 'an ugly or evil-looking old woman.' But this, considering the source, may be considered a compliment. For the beauty of strong, creative women is 'ugly' by misogynistic standards of 'beauty.'"

Daly concludes with a new spin on the "c-word." "For women who have transvaluated this, a Crone is one who should be an example of strength, courage and wisdom."

"Witch."

"Hag."

"Crone."

"Slut."

"Feminist."

There is alchemy within these words.

If language can be used to suppress dissent against arbitrary and abusive authority—and to name and vilify outsiders—then perverting and reclaiming language can be used to challenge those very systems of oppression. You can't take words out of the mouths of oppressors, but you can subvert the intended meaning of their words.

As philosopher and gender theorist Judith Butler explains in *Excitable Speech: A Politics of the Performative*, linguistic slurs and hate speech develop through repetition over years and years. Each person who has said "slut" or "witch" with cruel intentions breathes new life into the sexist discourse that imbues these words with their destructive potential.

To Butler, shying away from such words isn't the answer. "There is no purifying language of its traumatic residue," she writes, "and no way to work through trauma except through the arduous effort it takes to direct the course of its repetition."

It is always an imperfect process, but when women use terms like "witch" and "slut" strategically—and repeatedly—they can help remove the sting of savage history that lies within their syllables.

"Insurrectionary speech becomes the necessary response to injurious language, a risk taken in response to being put at risk, a repetition in language that forces change," Butler asserts.

Writing and uttering contested words can be a tool to subvert patriarchal rule. It is as much a political act as it is a radical ritual: a spell. Feminist magic, if you will.

"A spell is a symbolic act done in an altered state of consciousness, in order to cause a desired change," explains Starhawk.

And reappropriating language with a dedicated ethic can create change:

"Queer" was once a derogatory term for gay people, but because of the gay community's collective action to wrest it away from bigots, it is now embraced as an umbrella term for anyone who doesn't identify as cisgender and/or heterosexual.

Similarly, "dyke" was once an epithet used to describe gay women, but is now proudly voiced by lesbians around the world.

In *Coming to Power*, a collection of lesbian S/M writing first published in 1981, contributor Kitt likens reclaiming words to creating art: "Like an unfinished sculpture, the clay of many words is taken into the hands of women, feminists, lesbians for remolding. A multitude of Pandoras is opening up the confining boxes of words and images, letting them out to permeate every crevice of life, to no longer suffocate in compartments created by men, created to keep us in our place. We are reclaiming and remodeling words used to describe us, words used to belittle our bodies and sexuality: woman, mother, bitch, whore, frigid, aggressive, cunt, pussy. And in the process, we are reclaiming our lives."

To create a reclamation spell, all you need is intention, words, and repetition to conjure a desired outcome into being. This act can be for yourself alone or practiced in the name of all those who have suffered from pejorative language and hate speech.

The next step?

Crafting a language of our own creation.

Conceptual artist and founder of the Cliteracy project Sophia Wallace advocates moving beyond the trend of naming feminist movements (the SlutWalk) or feminist art shows (Nasty Women) after derogatory slurs women have received. "Why do we have to spend all of our time reacting?" Wallace inquired on a *Huffington Post*/*Bustle* panel about the role of artists in contemporary society. "Let's make new language. Instead of asking, 'Is she a slut,' the question really should be 'Are you *ill-cliterate*?'"

By forging a new lexicon, women can center their experiences without stumbling over the vestiges of abuse harbored within patriarchal syllables.

"The tongue is a witch," Anglican minister George Webbe famously said in 1619. And witches, sluts, and feminists are wielding its formidable power with magic in mind.

SEX MAGIC & THE TOOLS OF PLEASURE

Sex was the X factor in the witch trials. *The Malleus Malefi-carum* decreed witchcraft was afoot when a woman was exceedingly amorous and dared to publicly express as much—or when a man couldn't perform sexually. There was no room for female sexual pleasure in church doctrine, only procreation. In fact, any whiff of enjoyment outside reproduction was condemned.

Heinrich Kramer singled out "female fornicators" as the type of women who were "frequently sorceresses." Even before the tome's publication, stories were spun regarding witches perverting the domestic tools of womanhood to pleasure themselves—and to fly through the air to their orgiastic sabbaths. Female sexuality, on its own, separate from men, was an abomination—and an obsession—during the witch hunts. And so the debate was sparked:

Was the witch's broom a dust buster, transportation device, or dildo?

In extant documents from the 1324 trials of Ireland's first accused witch, Lady Alice Kyteler, inquisitors describe finding her special stash of flying ointment. "In rifleing the closet of the ladie, they found a pipe of oyntment, wherewith she greased a staffe, upon which she ambled and galloped through thick and thin," they write.

Imagine being arrested after the cops found your Hitachi Magic Wand?*

Less than a hundred years after Lady Alice's dildo was taken as evidence of her witchery, the broom-as-sex-toy discourse found its way into visual art.

An unattributed woodcut from c. 1400 depicts a witch, demon, and warlock incoming on their broomsticks toward a peasant woman. Ulrich Molitor's 1489 etchings star a few strange beasts riding backward on a cooking fork, and Albrecht Dürer's c. 1500 "Witch Riding Backwards on a Goat" shows a broom slipped between a sorceress' thighs.

Richard Cavendish drops another morsel of masturbation intrigue in *The Black Arts: A Concise History of Witchcraft, Demonology, Astrology, and Other Mystical Practices throughout the Ages*. He details accused witch of Savoy Antoine Rose's broomstick confession under torture in 1477.

After she supposedly made a deal with the Devil, the dark one "gave her a stick eighteen inches long and a jar of ointment. She would smear the stick with the ointment, put it between her legs and say, 'Go in the Devil's name, go!' and immediately be carried through the air."

Beyond such carnal accounts, this diabolical ointment has also been studied for its hallucinatory qualities.

Michael Pollan discloses in *The Botany of Desire: A Plant's-Eye View of the World* that midwives, herbalists, and ladies in the know (aka witches) would cultivate "psychoactive" agents including datura, opium poppies, belladona, hashish, and even the skin of toads with trace levels of the hallucinogen DMT. "These ingredients would be combined in a hempseed-oil-based 'flying ointment' that the witches would then administer vaginally using a special dildo," he writes. "This was the 'broomstick' by which these women were said to travel."

We will never know for certain the extent to which the broomstick was a metaphorical or metaphysical device.

---

* This could conceivably happen in Alabama today, where sex toys remain illegal.

To some witches, masturbation can be an act of sex magic, where the energy raised during arousal and release is tantamount to spellcasting, and a specific goal can be achieved in the throes of ecstasy. As Margot Anand asserts in *The Art of Sexual Magic*, "any vision or desire that you wish to manifest in your life needs to be charged with your orgasmic sexual power."

Intimate spellcasting can indeed take many shapes.

But sometimes a broom is just a broom.

For Chakrubs founder and witch Vanessa Cuccia, the sex toy remains a transformative, healing object that is both spiritual and sexual. Instead of dealing in brooms, however, she deals in crystals.

After feasting her eyes on an enchanting crystal wand at a friend's house, Cuccia told *Slutist* in 2015 that she suddenly had "the aha moment to masturbate with crystals."

"I wanted to have crystals inside. In my mouth, in my bra, in my pussy," she said. "It felt like an urge to have my body be filled with crystal."

Since 2011, Cuccia has been selling 100 percent pure crystal sexual wellness products through her company Chakrubs. With the goal of bringing "a sense of sacredness to your playtime," these objets d'art can be used in a variety of ways.

Designed with the practice of crystal healing in mind, Chakrubs' products can be charged under a full moon to activate their potential. Each crystal has a different energetic purpose that users can learn about from the company's website. Rose quartz, for example, can work on "dissolving emotional wounds, fears and resentments," amethyst can "bring emotional stability and inner strength," and black obsidian can "absorb negative energy and help to release mental stress and promote emotional well-being." Chakrubs' fetish- and weapon-inspired Shadow Line is crafted predominantly with black obsidian and stainless steel, and users are ecouraged to employ these "interactive sculptures" to delve into the darkness we all carry within.

It's the rare sex toy that aims to erase both boundaries between the sacred and the profane and the shame surrounding female sexual pleasure.

"Crystals are something magical I can touch," Cuccia said. "I prefer to practice my spirituality in very practical ways. And I know for many crystals don't seem practical, but to me it is clear the magic they hold. I can feel the energy pulsing through them into my hand when I hold them. Crystals make sense to me. They are grounded, they come from the earth."

Whether you embrace the healing properties of crystals or just like the idea of a sleek, all-natural sexual aide, Chakrubs offers much to the modern, sex-positive witch.

In the 1950s, the work of sexologist Alfred Kinsey helped to slowly initiate a societal conversation about female masturbation. Sixty-two percent of women in his 1953 study *Sexuality in the Human Female* admitted to pleasuring themselves, and although he found that masturbation was the second most common sexual practice of women, it was the single practice where orgasm was most likely achieved. Despite Kinsey's publicized findings, the pushback by conservative religious groups against masturbation—female masturbation in particular—continued via campaigns spreading misinformation and sex-negative distortions.

Over fifty years later, masturbation stigma persists, but science is now more than ever on the side of self-pleasure. A variety of studies have enumerated the connections between masturbation and self-esteem, sexual health, and positive body image for women, and there are an increasing number of entrepreneurs such as Cuccia who seek to challenge centuries of sexual repression through their sexual products.

To explore the links between self-pleasure and contempo-

rary witchcraft, I interviewed a witch-identified woman who recently experimented with a "flying ointment" she sourced on-line. On condition of anonymity, she revealed her very personal experience with this psychedelic salve.

It's amazing now with the internet all the ways you can connect with fellow witches around the world. I was linked by a friend to a woman who created a flying ointment in Spain. She grows her own henbane, mandrake, belladonna, and datura, and she fertilizes it under the full moon with her menstrual blood. She's very intentional about creating this substance, packages it beautifully, and sells it on Etsy.

Because I don't have much of a green thumb, I thought I would just get it and keep it on my altar. I sat with it for two years before I actually got around to doing it because I didn't feel like it was the right time. I had a beautiful experience with it actually, feeling very connected to the energy of the plant, feeling like it was giving me a new lens with which to understand the universe and have this dialogue with the plant, the spirit of the plant, whatever you want to call it.

It was kind of saying it was now part of my vocabulary and was going to be informing my thought processes and my understanding of things going forward, even when I'm not actively taking it. It was very different than other psychedelic plants. It's technically a deliriant and not a psychedelic. It's part of a different chemical family with a different way of acting on the body.

I was reading about the witch's ointment and the idea of witches riding broomsticks and how it's still debated about whether it took place or not. Either it was slander by the church or it was real, and even if it was just slander, it's still fascinating because we're scared of women humping broomsticks and getting high. Sex and drugs are so threatening to our society, and in particular women's sexuality and women having access to altered states.

It did feel like a real reclaiming to be rubbing that ointment on my pussy.

THE SPELL OF SEDUCTION: SEX WORK & THE SACRED WHORE

Like the witches of legend who could summon a sudden downpour, some witches of today can summon the forces to make it rain at the strip club. They can transform a single session of bondage and domination into a transformative ritual. They can invoke passion and healing all in one evening. Whether conjuring the elements or crisp $100s, such acts require working with potent, unseen energies.

"My experiences in sex work played a big part in me beginning to identify as a witch," explains Eve G., a sex worker and healer. "I was coming into my own sexual power, as well as realizing my ability to perceive and transmit energetically when I was with my clients. I began to seek out new language for what I was experiencing, to explore new paradigms that didn't exclude my experiences."

At the nexus of the witch and slut identities is sex work. Some women who choose to work in the sex industry—as strippers, porn performers, dominatrixes—see their practice as part of a lineage of healers tapping into taboo female power.

For Yin Q., a writer, BDSM educator, and self-identified "shamanatrix," energy work plays a central role in her practice with clients. "I incorporate personal rituals of ancestral acknowledgment, Taoist meditations, and animism to create 'walls' for the circle prior to the session so I have my own pillars to call upon for my part to play in the ritual," she says. "My service to the community is as a guide and provider of safe space for individuals to tap into energy work and magic through BDSM play."

Siouxsie Q., author and sex workers' rights advocate, has examined the connection between the witch identity and sex work for her *SF Weekly* column, *The Whore Next Door*. "In a capitalist patriarchal society, women who have the power to make men give them money through their own mysterious magic is a terrifying proposition that threatens to dismantle everything," she writes.

To produce an altered state of consciousness through raising and releasing primal desires is to be versed in the art of shifting reality and perception. Weaving a spell of seduction, like any spell, requires an intimacy with the physical and the metaphysical realms.

In the twenty-first century, however, this work is roundly maligned. Sex workers in America are four hundred times more likely to be murdered on the job than other workers, and women of color and trans women are disproportionately affected by this violence. According to statistics released by the Sex Workers Outreach Project in 2015, 41 percent of sex workers killed were black, and 29 percent were transgender. Sex work remains criminalized in the United States, and those seeking respite from abuse via police intervention can therefore be arrested, sexually assaulted, or coerced into providing their services to escape punishment.

It's important to emphasize that not all sex workers have the luxury of choosing their profession, and that not all view it uncritically. Regardless of the nuanced factors that motivate each individual to enter and stay in the industry, however, sex workers are persecuted both by the patriarchal authorities and by the feminist narratives that conflate sex work with sex trafficking.

Just as women who defied the sexual status quo were once persecuted as witches, sex workers are persecuted for using their bodies to survive and even thrive in a culture that still has not granted complete bodily autonomy to women.

Sex work, however, has not always been so feared and despised.

Uniting the spiritual and the sexual like no other historical figure is the "sacred whore." Such women were priestesses in places like ancient Mesopotamia, Greece, and India who served as the living expression of the goddess of love over whose temple they presided. Through sexual congress with these women, worshippers could reach higher states of religious connection.

As Merlin Stone explains in *When God Was a Woman*, these priestesses had the ability to sire divine ecstasy with their lovers. "In the worship of the female deity, sex was Her gift to humanity. It was sacred and holy. She was the Goddess of Sexual Love and Procreation," she writes.

The sacred whore is an archetype found in both myths and historical documents. Her particulars are a continued source of scholarly debate. Evidence of the sacred whore can be found in *The Code of Hammurabi*, the Babylonian laws from c. 1754 BC that spell out special protections for temple prostitutes, and in Greek historian Herodotus' fifth-century BC *Histories*, which include a disdainful mention of sex rituals occurring at the temple of Ishtar, the goddess of fertility, love, war, and sex.

Mesopotamian, Syrian, and Hebrew texts also link terms for sacred women with prostitution. Some suggest these links prove the sacred whore's primacy. Others say it's an error of translation.

Eve G. became fascinated by this shadowy history after intuiting her shared path with these priestesses. "My personal understanding came to me astride a client. It was a completely embodied realization that, 'whoah, I am not the first woman to experience this healing and spiritual role, there must be some kind of lineage here.'"

As the records remain spotty on the subject, it's up to laypeople and historians alike to discern the bias and intentions of those writing about sacred whoredom over the years.

"When I write or talk about the sacred whore, it's more through myth and archetype," writer and educator Britta Love explains, "because even though I personally believe sacred whores existed in history, or at least that sex work was constructed in ways that do not reflect the sacred/profane duality Western culture holds today, after years of researching I can tell you we don't have it all figured out yet. The evidence of actual sacred whores in academic and historical writing is very difficult to parse because of the historiographic problem of Western and patriarchal social biases. Late nineteenth-century writers were talking about primitive people having orgies in the temples. Later on you have a second-wave feminist revision that the sacred whore is a male fantasy objectifying women, and then there's this cynical modern lens, which is that there was sex in the temples, but it was purely exploitative to raise money for the temple."

When looking at the connections between sexuality and spirituality, however, proof isn't always the point.

"What I do know for certain is that this archetype has informed the work of a lot of modern sex workers," Love concludes, "so if it wasn't real back then, it certainly is now."

QUEERING THE WITCH: PORN, PLEASURE & REPRESENTATION

"Society's dread of women who own their desire, and use it in ways that confound expectations of proper female sexuality, persists."

—*The Feminist Porn Book*

From a contemporary perspective, early modern depictions of witches cavorting naked with limbs entwined are unquestionably queer. In Hans Baldung Grien's "New Year's Wish with Three Witches" from c. 1514, a young witch with untamed hair fondles her vulva while a crone caresses the back of another young witch crouching on all fours. This may scream hot, intergenerational lesbian threesome to us, but to God-fearing men of the day, it symbolized demonic sexuality first and foremost.

Sapphic signifiers abound in portrayals of the witch.

Sherry Velasco explains in *Lesbians in Early Modern Spain* that "the eroticized body of the witch in sixteenth- and seventeenth-century images revealed both a voyeuristic interest in female sexuality and a fear of women appropriating male sexual power." Some witch imagery was also giving voice to "deep-seated male fears of lesbian sexuality, with its threat of impotence and castration," she adds.

There are few recorded instances of lesbian witches during the European trials, but "evidence is scant but suggestive," says Anne Barstow in *Witchcraze*. She details a lurid—yet part-

warming—tale of one French mother superior accused of witch-craft for performing cunnilingus and seducing other nuns with a strap-on. Lyndal Roper affirms in *Witch Craze* that lesbian witch accusations were rarely documented but notes one Protestant tract that warned of lesbian witches ensnaring naive, unsuspecting wives. As the men creating anti-witch narratives were presumably heterosexual, Satanic sex was most frequently characterized as penetrative, between a female witch and a male Devil.

The witch has always embodied the sexual fears of men, whether they be of women finding sexual pleasure without them, emasculating them, or castrating them. Portrayals of the woman-as-witch have thus reflected an unquenchable desire for the female sex mixed with fear, straddling horror and pleasure, disgust and arousal.

Today, pornography is one site where the battle for female sexual representation is being fought. Some women have the privilege of creating their own sexual representations for the spectator of their choosing—one who isn't by default a cisgender, heterosexual male—while others are harnessing or subverting the traditional male gaze for their own devices.

Despite this, pornography remains anathema to many feminists. The so-called "Feminist Sex Wars" that began percolating in the late 1970s reached their zenith in the 1980s and produced two ideological camps: anti-porn feminists and pro-sex or anti-censorship feminists. The former believed the misogyny inherent in mainstream pornography and explicit media promotes rape and sexism and should be stopped at all costs—and through government intervention when necessary. The latter believed that such a view amounts to sexual puritanism and promotes censorship, and that consensual sexual expression in all forms should be a protected right.

During this deep ideological conflict, feminist pornography as a genre began to flesh out, and the sex-positive feminist movement solidified around the idea that sexual freedom is a fundamental human right, and it is up to each individual to decide what consensual sexual expression means to them.

In the early 1980s, Candida Royalle started Femme Productions "to put a woman's voice to adult movies." Susie Bright
co-founded the lesbian porn magazine *On Our Backs*, and Annie Sprinkle blurred the lines between feminism, activism, performance art, and porn. Thirty years on, they and sex-positive
feminists like them have mainstreamed the discourse on sexual
pleasure, sex workers' rights, and BDSM.

Contemporary feminism remains fractured on issues of
porn, sex work, and sexual representation, but feminist porn is
more visible than ever. For those who prefer their smut served
with a side of ethics and empowerment, feminist porn is an
overarching term for productions that often pay fair wages;
showcase actors of disparate races, ages, abilities, and gender
expressions; and depict fantasies and plot lines that promote tit-
illation and fantasy from a woman's and/or queer person's perspective. You might have stumbled upon feminist porn if the
female orgasm is queen, gender is fluid, squirting is celebrated,
and/or non-normative bodies are normalized.

Attempting to define the slippery subject that is feminist porn, author, activist, and feminist pornographer Tristan
Taormino once likened it to the organic food movement. The
product is important, but the means of production is equally so,
she stressed. But although feminist porn can indeed challenge
the very sexism, exploitation, and dehumanization that some
feminists suggest mainstream pornography perpetuates, that
doesn't mean mainstream porn is monolithically problematic
and should be off-limits for any self-respecting feminist.

"Can we watch sexist porn and still have feminist or-
gasms?" asks author and professor Jane Ward in *The Feminist
Porn Book*. Yes, she answers, but mindfulness is key to enjoying
any kind of questionable media. "Lucky are those whose arousal
results from homegrown and independently produced feminist
porn cast with gender-variant people of various races, body siz-
es, and abilities," Ward writes. "But for some of us, mainstream
porn—for all of its sexist and racist tropes and questionable labor practices—still casts its spell."

And some of those very spell casters happen to be witches. In addition to being a sex-positive feminist pioneer, AVN Hall of Famer and witch Annie Sprinkle has starred in both mainstream and feminist pornography. She is also one of the first adult entertainers to publicly celebrate the intersection between alternative spirituality and sex.

Whether hosting sex magic group rituals or honoring the ancient history of the sacred whore on film and in performance, Sprinkle, a "fearless sex slut," has infused divine connection into her porn, workshops, and performance art for decades.

Bailey Jay, a self-described "transsexual porn star witch," is a young performer who has won multiple Adult Video News Awards. As Jay explained in an interview with *Motherboard*, her ability to express herself and abandon inhibitions on camera correlates with her personal magical practice. "It feels good to have a relationship with your God," she said. "If you have a very liberal job, you probably have a very liberal mindset, you're not rigid. So I feel like it makes sense. If I have a job where I feel free enough to be naked and have sex on camera. I might also be free enough to worship nature, or not feel stupid worshipping God."

Both pornography and witchcraft thrive in the liminal space between fantasy and reality, which might explain why there are a number of former and current porn performers who identify as witches or occultists. Performing in porn and practicing witchcraft require working with instinctual desires to create palpable energetic shifts, and those involved in each can face societal stigma for their work.

Like many representations of female sexuality, the wanton witches depicted in early modern art were designed to be consumed hungrily with a certain level of disgust for the sinners in frame, and there are plenty of porn watchers who consume adult films in a similar way. For the first time in history, however, female sexuality is not solely portrayed with the leering eyes of the patriarchy in mind, and when it is, the performers are often aware of and capitalizing on this dynamic. As feminist actors and producers of contemporary pornography continue to foreground their own pleasure and power, many are using their magic, be it literal or figurative, to pleasure and empower their diverse audiences in the process.

Because of strides made by the sex-positive and feminist movements over the past fifty years, there is more freedom in America to focus on female sexual desire in both the public and private spheres—and women are doing so in witchy ways.

Atlanta-based "stripper with a PhD" and atheist feminist Lux ATL uses the witch archetype to heal many women the deep wounds of sexist conditioning and sexual repression. She designed her *Stripcraft Spellbook* as a method for women to embrace and fully embody their sexuality. The multi-media course is "one part feminist philosophy and one part stripper-style dance school," and encourages participants to shake off the shackles of patriarchy one move at a time.

In an interview with *Dirge Magazine* Lux explained that she uses the witch as a metaphor "to encourage cultural blasphemy and subversion" in her work. "The Witch represents notions of a strange, unconventional, frighteningly powerful womanhood," Lux stated. "She is servant to no one."

Others take the connection between sexual empowerment and the witch to a spiritual level.

Courses on sex magic, sacred sexuality, and sexual enhancement are frequent offerings at occult shops and wellness centers around the country. Vanessa Cuccia, Annie Sprinkle, and Britta Love are just a few aforementioned examples of sex-positive witches offering their slice of spiritual and sexual scholarship to folks with an open mind and a willingness to learn.

But despite the important work of these women and others like them, sexual stigma persists.

In a historical first, President Obama spoke out about this omnipresent issue, addressing the sexual double standards that have plagued women since well before the witch trials.

"We need to change the attitude that punishes women for their sexuality," he said during the 2016 White House Summit on the United States of Women, "but gives men a pat on the back for theirs." A month later, the president outed himself as a feminist in an article he wrote for *Glamour* magazine, doubling down on his previous proclamation.

For the most prominent and powerful American politician to take issue with deep rooted, sexual oppression—and to call himself a feminist—was revolutionary. At a time when countless politicians are looking to silence the gains made by feminism and to keep female sexuality and female sexual health in the dark ages, this statement had impact. Given the dramatic shift in America's leadership since then, it's difficult to know just how much this view will be undermined and actively suppressed. But it was nevertheless a hopeful moment that will not soon be forgotten, full of possibility, for witches, sluts, and feminists everywhere.

UNDRESSING THE WITCH: FASHION, STYLE & SARTORIAL SPELLS

"The original witches were benevolent but because people didn't understand them they bullied them. We're left with a bad image of them."
> —Rei Kawakubo, Comme des Garçons

"If sluttiness is what you like, what's wrong with that? Why do we think being a slut's bad? Sluttiness is just a lot of freedom."
> —Tom Ford

In Puritan New England, sumptuary laws defined what proper, God-fearing folk should wear. Designations about the cut and color of clothing were enforced with economic and regulatory functions in mind. They kept rich and poor in their place by linking compliance with godliness, and they also signaled who was a sinner—and who was a witch.

The 1651 Colonial Laws of Massachusetts expressly forbid "silk or tiffany hoods, or scarves" to be worn by women of lower classes, despite being "allowable to persons of greater estates or more liberal education." During the Salem witch trials, when Tituba accused two lower-class women of being witches alongside her, she noted that they were wearing finery above their status. She spoke of a tall Devil dressed in black they encountered, and in the next breath said the other witches appeared in "a black silk hood with a white silk hood under it."

Tituba knew what she was doing, according to Elaine G. Breslaw in *Tituba, Reluctant Witch of Salem: Devilish Indians and Puritan Fantasies*. By describing these women in such a fashion, she provided a "veiled reference to respectability" in "an attempt to identify maleficium with higher social status." To keep herself alive in a world that treated her inhumanely, Tituba seemed to align sartorial transgression with devilry, which aligned with Puritanical thinking at the time.

Sartorial transgression would also be the downfall of Bridget Bishop, the first woman to be executed during the Salem witch trials. She was convicted in part because she was seen gallivanting about in a red bodice and acting in a boisterous manner. As traditional Puritan garb was dominated by muted tones, this flashy hue set Bishop apart. She had previously been accused and acquitted of witchcraft after her second husband died suddenly.

In the deposition of Salem resident William Stacy in 1692, he swore under oath that Bishop bewitched him in his room late one night while wearing her signature scarlet garment. Although many historians today believe Bridget was confused and conflated by "witnesses" with local tavern keeper Sarah Bishop, another accused witch, Bridget was the one hanged.

In Salem lore, she remains known as the witch in red.

Hundreds of years later, fashion stills speaks louder than words. The length of a hemline, the tightness of a blouse, or the style of undergarments has been used in courts to sway juries to believe a victim of sexual assault was "asking for it" through her outfit. This evidence has been enough to acquit an accused rapist.

In the *Yale Journal of Law & Feminism*, Alinor C. Sterling explains how the defense uses clothing in a case.

"While prosecutors often use clothing evidence to prove penetration, force, and other physical facts at issue in a rape case, defense attorneys may offer the same clothing as proof of the mental states of both the defendant and the victim," she writes.

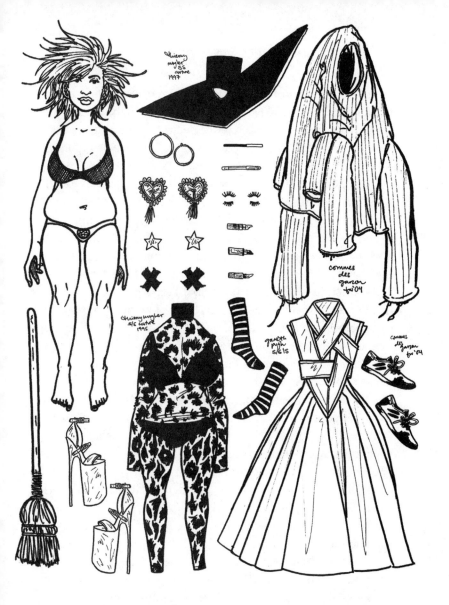

"For example, the defense may suggest that revealing clothing is relevant to a determination of the reasonableness of the defendant's belief that the victim consented. If the victim invited the defendant to her house and opened the door wearing a negligee, the defense attorney might argue that her clothing supported the defendant's reasonable belief that she was consenting to sex," Sterling concludes.

Even when clothing is excised from evidence—as it was in Florida after a 1990 law barred citing a woman's clothing in sexual assault cases unless a judge deems it necessary—what a woman was wearing during a rape or sexual assault is still up for discussion.

"I've been told I'm not supposed to say this. . . . [W]omen should avoid dressing like sluts in order not to be victimized," said a Toronto police officer in 2011, inspiring the first SlutWalk.

Although the SlutWalk movement is about far more than a woman's clothing style, a comment about clothing provided the spark for the movement to catch fire. As the founders of SlutWalk Toronto Heather Jarvis and Sonya Barnett expressed in their 2011 manifesto: "We are tired of being oppressed by slut-shaming; of being judged by our sexuality and feeling unsafe as a result. Being in charge of our sexual lives should not mean that we are opening ourselves to an expectation of violence, regardless if we participate in sex for pleasure or work. No one should equate enjoying sex with attracting sexual assault."

Kaitlynn Mendes explains in *SlutWalk: Feminism, Activism, and Media* how "the movement has been shaped by its geographical and temporal settings, local issues, current events and organizers' personal understanding of sexual violence and rape culture." No two SlutWalks are identical, but they all work to challenge contemporary victim-blaming discourses around sexual assault—and often feature women in various states of undress for political ends.

The SlutWalk ethos affirms that no person, regardless of gender, race, job, or fashion choice asks to be assaulted. Sex workers aren't asking for it. Women in crop tops aren't asking for it. Women in miniskirts aren't asking for it. Women in hoodies aren't asking for it.

Clothing has been used as an excuse to hang women for witchcraft and to sexually assault them for centuries, but clothing has also been a source of empowerment for women, offering a visible threat to gender norms.

Some witches cast off their clothes to work skyclad, unencumbered by fashion. Others outfit themselves in layer upon layer to enhance their magic. Although clothes don't necessarily make the witch, her inimitable aesthetic is everywhere.

Concocted out of history, myth, and movies, witch style belongs to no single culture. A witch can be draped in a kimono or wrapped in tribal prints. She can be done up in medieval, Renaissance, Victorian, or Edwardian finery. She can be profoundly stylish or oddly out of season. Sometimes, the way a woman wears her clothing more than what she is actually wearing betrays her witchiness.

But most often, we think of the witch cloaked in darkness—all in black.

Decades ago, the witch infiltrated high fashion and never left. Designers like Thierry Mugler, Ann Demeulemeester, Yohji Yamamoto, Gareth Pugh, and countless others have looked to her for inspiration year after year.

In 2004, Comme des Garçons' Rei Kawakubo described her new witch-inspired collection to *Dazed* magazine. The Japanese designer explicitly linked the witch with a history of strength and resilience.

"I was thinking about witches," she said. "Witches in the original sense of the word, in the sense of a woman having power. The original witches were benevolent, but because people didn't understand them they bullied them. We're left with a bad image of them."

The clothes Kawakubo produced for that year's fall collection were black and grey, with ruffles and furs, leather and bows. The models wore a streak of bright red lipstick on half their mouths, with hair twisted into snake-like shapes atop their heads.

In 2015, the witch was back in a Comme des Garçons collection, this time in rich greys, blacks, and blues with asymmetrical, voluminous cuts. Barely any skin was revealed on the runway, save for the models' faces and their shocks of fire engine red hair.

Kawakubo's design partner and husband Adrian Joffe encapsulated the collection to *Dazed* magazine once more, echoing her earlier sentiments: "Witches. These are strong women that are often misunderstood by the world," he said.

During the witch-hunting era, the word "glamour" meant a magic spell, an illusion fabricated by a witch. Now, it refers to an aesthetic practice that many women embrace, whether a surface transformation tailored through makeup and fashion or something far more spellbinding.

To delve deeper into the sexual power and subversive sartorial expressions of the witch, I spoke with author, fashion historian, and Director of the Museum at FIT Valerie Steele.

"We know historically that most of the women who were executed as witches were older women who were vilified and scapegoated," says Steele. "I do think that in the sexy fashion images you compare the younger, Lolita-like princess with the older maleficent witch who is sexually mature and a phallic figure."

This "phallic woman," she explains, embodies the popular male fantasy of the powerful, sexually dominant woman. Steele references the dominatrixes she interviewed for her book *Fetish: Fashion, Sex & Power*.

"They talked about how high heels and corsets and high hair and anything that makes you a hard, tall, and dominant-looking figure reinforces the power differential, but also emphasizes the power of erotic femininity."

But although the witch-as-phallic-woman is erotically charged, this doesn't translate to scantily clad.

"We tend to think nowadays that sexuality is expressed in body exposure," Steele points out. "However, people who have thought about sex ranging from Casanova to Freud have talked a lot about the attraction of concealment. So the idea of having the body all covered often takes its cue from a neo-Victorian aesthetic." And within that aesthetic, black is a mercurial shade, used to signify everything from sexy evil to mourning. "Black has such a powerful range of meanings," Steele affirms.

Like the witch, the slut is ever present on the catwalk, too. While more fabric often means more witchy, leaving less to the imagination is the slut's job.

Slut fashion is slightly trickier to pin down, but it is most often a designation given to clothing that's barely there—or that incorporates the signifiers of wild animals: leopard, cheetah, snake, zebra. These become the surrogate skins of untamed women.

In 2013, *T Magazine* heralded the end of slut style. Fashion critic Suzy Menkes wrote: "Out of Italy has come a fashion miracle: a look that suddenly puts 'la moda da puttana' ('hooker chic') right out of vogue." Instead, she praised high button collars, long skirts, and long sleeves.

Steele says that to her knowledge, "prostitute fashion" has only ever been a derogatory term—a critique frequently leveled at Versace, for example.

Concealed or revealed, witch or slut, these style archetypes can express aspects of female sexuality that are not incongruous with feminism. What makes fashion empowering or feminist has far less to do with the clothing itself than with the intent of the wearer. It is up to the individual to decide how her wardrobe may or may not promote her politics or reflect her gender identity. Style remains a powerful signifier, and contemporary American women have more ability than ever to transform their bodies through fashion from the property of patriarchy into vessels of dissent.

"Old-school feminists saw [feminism and fashion] as anathema," Steele states. But by the third wave, the idea of fashion as a woman's avenue for self-expression began to gain credence. Now, fashion is just as likely to be viewed as "empowering, individualist, and expressive—not just a Moloch that destroys women," she concludes.

WITCHCRAFT ON SCREEN: LIVING DELICIOUSLY

"The whole history of witchcraft is interwoven with the fear of female sexuality. They burned us at the stake because they feared the erotic feelings we elicited in them."

—*The Love Witch*

"Wouldst thou like to live deliciously?"

—*The Witch*

Whether a wizened crone or a feral femme fatale, the witch-as-villain is seared into our imaginations from early childhood. From Maleficent to Mater Suspiriorum to Bellatrix Lestrange, she is the woman we love to emulate or fear. These archetypal depictions are addicting to watch, and are often an expression of the "monstrous-feminine," which reflects male anxieties about the female body.

According to film theorist Barbara Creed, "The presence of the monstrous-feminine in the popular horror film speaks to us more about male fears than about female desire or feminine subjectivity." And as witchcraft propaganda from the early modern era set forth, when women are monstrous, their evil most often emanates from their sexuality and reproductive function.

One of the earliest examples of the witch's villainous

carnality is in *Häxan: Witchcraft Throughout the Ages*. The 1922 Swedish film first pairs images of witches from medieval works of art accompanied by text about early European witchcraft beliefs. *Häxan* then breaks into a live action sequence that features malicious acts of spellcasting, Satanic analingus, bedding Beelzebub, and lubing up lasciviously with flying ointment.

As the medium of film developed in complexity, the monstrous witch became an animated favorite. In Disney classics, the witch is an aging woman pitted against a dewy ingénue. Both *Snow White and the Seven Dwarfs* and *Sleeping Beauty* depict generational clashes between old witches and young beauties, pegging a woman's worth on fertility and youth—never hard-won wisdom.

The monstrous-feminine isn't complete without forbidden sex appeal, however, which always comes with a dash of castration anxiety. In Creed's analysis of the trope, she refers to the 1960 film *Black Sunday*, which stars Barbara Steele as both a demure woman from a cursed family as well as the frightening witch who has cursed them. At the climax of the film, the male protagonist cannot tell the difference between the two—one, his love interest, and the other, a source of evil in the Moldavian village they inhabit. The extended metaphor for woman as two-faced seductress plays out exquisitely with the leading man at his wits' end trying to figure out which woman is witch.

When the feminist movement first gained visibility in the early 1960s, the witch began to transcend her evil origins. Whether this was a coincidence, a reflection of women's liberation, or an attempt to declaw the witch and offer a kinder, gentler sorceress is difficult to say. Nevertheless, the first major pop culture witch in this category (post-Glinda, of course) is Samantha Stephens from *Bewitched*.

Samantha made her bouncy blonde debut one year after the 1963 publication of Betty Friedan's *The Feminine Mystique*, which galvanized the women's liberation movement by uncovering "the problem that has no name"—the plight of white, middle-class housewives under the crushing thumb of patriarchy.

Five episodes of *Bewitched* were written by self-described feminist Barbara Avedon, and despite its bourgeois trappings, the show did present an alternate take on gender roles that was forward-thinking for its time.

In the first episode of the show, Samantha confesses her powers to new husband Darrin, only to be told never to use them again—because they scare the hell out of him. She reluctantly agrees, but soon after, while staring with frustration at a messy kitchen, she wiggles her nose and *poof!* Domestic duties done.

Samantha uses witchcraft throughout the series to manage both personal and professional issues, much to the chagrin of her husband, who often wishes she would behave like a "normal" woman.

Magic thus functions in *Bewitched* as an apt metaphor for feminism—knowledge with the potential for personal empowerment and transformation that is feared and forbidden by the patriarchs.

As the '60s wore on, the witch became more nuanced. Some portrayals held her up as a feminist hero, while others played upon her classic monstrosity. Most, however, did a little bit of both.

In 1987, *The Witches of Eastwick* bit back against puritanical sexual mores, but was still conventionally sexy in certain ways. The film, based on John Updike's novel of the same name, follows three friends who discover their magic abilities. They initially let their lust for the same man (a thinly disguised Devil) come between them, but soon give up on jealousy and join together in a polyamorous quad relationship of sorts. Countering the age-old narrative of witches seduced by Satan and forever under his spell, these women use the Devil for sex and procreation before casting him out of their circle for good.

Nearly a decade later, *The Craft* was released to great success, garnering induction into the canon of teen witch feminism. A closer look, however, reveals an unsavory underbelly. The 1996 film depicts four young women discovering friendship and magic and banding together to fight their foes—before it all goes terribly, terribly wrong. What begins as a promising show of female bonding descends into a sexist circle jerk around the idea that girls just can't handle power.

As practicing witch and feminist writer Morgan Claire Sirene sums it up in her critique of *The Craft* for *Slutist*: "This film is a feminist nightmare masquerading as a cool subculture flick. When I say feminist nightmare, I mean the original feminists: Witches. This film isn't a celebration, it's a witch burning."

One of the most problematic characters is Nancy, the quintessential goth bad girl who suffers from a traumatic home life and has dealt with vicious slut-shaming at school. Eventually, she turns on her friends and becomes homicidal, killing the young jock who once spread rumors about her. Instead of being portrayed as wounded by toxic teen culture and lashing out in self-defense, Nancy is positioned as a villainous psychopath. Despite her abusive background, we are not meant to sympathize with this young woman. She ends up institutionalized at the film's end, and the good girl/bad girl binary marches on.

"It's just like every other misogynist work showcasing women as basket cases who can't handle power, sex or even friendship. They must be locked up or lead a more pious life," Sirene concludes.

But when women are in the writer's room, the witch often gains more dimension.

J.K. Rowling created Hermione Granger in her *Harry Potter* series (which was made into eight films) with reverence for the scholarship required to be a practicing witch. Despite being muggle born (without magical parents), Granger put a studious spin on engaging with spells and magic, which helps her rescue the men in her life, time and time again.

Screenwriter Linda Woolverton updated *Sleeping Beauty* in 2014 with a contemporary adaptation for Disney's *Maleficent*. Instead of merely following a witch hell bent on revenge, the tale touches upon love, betrayal, and platonic love between women. True love's kiss to awaken the bewitched princess comes from Maleficent, and the plot explicitly breaks through the "good witch/bad witch" binary, as the narrator names Maleficent "one who was both hero and villain" right before the credits roll.

One of the most adroit and self-aware depictions of the witch in recent years is Anna Biller's *The Love Witch*. Biller wrote, directed, edited, and produced the film, released in 2016, in the saturated style of a 1960s pulp thriller. Employing her own prismatic twist on the "monstrous feminine," the plot follows the trials of a stunning young woman who uses sex magick to make men fall in love with her. The protagonist, Elaine, sees less-than-ideal outcomes, however, and is left with blood on her hands.

Biller reveals in the director's statement for the independent film that she strove to create a work "about lived female experience that caters to women's visual pleasure." Crafting eye-catching costumes and props herself, Biller presents "the female image on film not as an image to be possessed, but as an image in the mirror." Throughout the course of *The Love Witch* she also manages to address romantic ideals, female sexual expression, and witch persecutions throughout history—while giving us a taste of a sex-positive pagan community—something few witch films have dared to do in such explicit ways.

"I think that women who know their own power are witches," Biller told *New Jack Witch*, "and also women who are artists are witches. I was not raised with any religion, but I believe in magic as a real force in the world."

While these are but a few women-helmed films that complicate hegemonic depictions of the witch, it would be wrongheaded to say that only women are capable of making feminist statements in cinema.

Erotic awakenings, misandrist fantasies, and a twist on classic cinematic tropes made Robert Eggers' *The Witch* a breakout feminist favorite in 2016. Although the film was informed by Christian witchcraft doctrine and was written and directed by a man, critics and theatergoers alike were drawn to its spark of subversive rebellion. Relying on period lighting to set a stark atmosphere and period texts to inform the fire and brimstone dialogue, *The Witch* largely let history speak for itself.

"I was trying to figure out what 'the witch' meant in the early modern period and depict 'the evil witch' in a way that she would have been understood in the time," Eggers told the *A.V. Club* in an interview. "But without any agendas, feminism rises to the top."

Reviews of the film were overwhelmingly glowing. They focused on how the plot of *The Witch* connected to current issues like fundamentalist religion or reproductive rights, and how it reified the witch as an evergreen symbol of feminist freedom.

However, some witch-identified women I interviewed felt the film only served to propagate dangerous stereotypes about female sexuality through the much maligned witch. In essence, the protagonist can't beat Satan, so she joins him, a capitulation to the idea that female sexuality is inherently deviant. This, they said, isn't liberation, but merely a choice the young girl makes to survive within the existing patriarchal system.

Whatever your view, *The Witch* does offer one ecstatic vision of an alternate universe for women to inhabit. A space to find sanctuary with other women unencumbered by God and patriarchy—a blood-soaked, clothing-optional, ladies-only occult paradise that's the stuff of misandrist, separatist wet dreams.

The true horror of Eggers' film is in the brutal redemption it portrays, depicting the worst fears of misogynists everywhere, perhaps best summed up by conservative Christian leader Pat Robertson back in the 1980s, when he decreed feminism a path for women to "leave their husbands, kill their children, practice witchcraft, destroy capitalism, and become lesbians."

As is often the case with popular media, *The Witch* is an imperfect political statement, but an important statement nonetheless.

"In the horror film," Barbara Creed explains, "the representation of the witch continues to foreground her essentially sexual nature." While centering sexuality is not a problem in itself, most characterizations—despite a few exceptions—play on sexist tropes, and are designed for a male viewer. As audiences demand nuanced content created with women in mind and female writers and directors gain funding and opportunities, witches are finally starting to exist on screen for more than just the male gaze. Although these witches may still serve to frighten and seduce, they also beg the question: What are we so afraid of—and why?

THE COVEN: CRAFTING FEMINIST COMMUNITY

Witches gathering deep in the woods conjuring mayhem inspired far more fear than solitary witches on the prowl. The "collective aspects" of witchcraft drove witch hysteria, according to John Demos in *The Enemy Within*—things like "shared rites, nocturnal meetings (the so-called *sabbat*) to renounce God and Christ, particular strategies of witch-to-witch recruitment, [and] the making of an explicit 'pact' with Satan."

Similar to the unholy witch covens imagined by men in early modern Europe, feminist consciousness-raising (CR) groups in the 1960s featured the most frightening thing of all—women united outside the company of men. What they did, what they said, and what they planned was a mystery to all but those involved.

These private, informal meet-ups where women were encouraged to open up about their struggles and desires helped crystallize the contemporary feminist movement. There, *The Feminine Mystique* and the feminine mystic began to coalesce.

Early CR groups usually took place in someone's residence, where "women gained the strength to challenge patriarchal forces at work and at home," bell hooks writes in *Feminism Is for Everybody*. Such a setting was ideal for intimate discussions about everything from workplace harassment and child rearing to the female orgasm. Whatever the women in each group chose to focus on, the meetings often took a nonhierarchical format in which longtime feminist thinkers and activists could share ideas with curious newcomers.

When the Goddess movement* began to gain popularity within feminist circles in the late 1960s, the witch and feminist worlds began to collide.

"The great lesson of CR was that personal feelings were to be trusted and acted upon, and that the personal was political," explains Wiccan priestess Margot Adler in *Drawing Down the Moon*. "The step from CR group to the coven was not long. Both are small groups that meet regularly and are involved in deeply personal questions. Only the focus differs."

Starhawk also uses the language of feminism to describe a coven in *The Spiral Dance*.

"The coven is a Witch's support group, consciousness-raising group, psychic study center," she writes, and its small size "makes it possible for rabid individualists to experience a deep sense of community without losing their independence of spirit."

As in a consciousness-raising group, much of what occurs between members in a coven is private, and only for the eyes and ears of those present. In fact, some covens never publicly share their existence to anyone outside their membership. Although the workings of such covens are better detailed in grimoires and spiritual guides, there is a new kind of coven on the rise.

These feminist groups may or may not follow a codified spiritual path, but still tap into the ancient practice of women gathering to create community and create change.

Girl Cvlt is a feminist activist group with a secret yet powerful internet presence that has grown to more than five thousand members worldwide. Although much of its activity is online, Girl Cvlt made headlines in 2016 when members

---

* The Goddess movement developed in the late 1960s as a response to male-dominated religions. The neo-pagan practice has no central tenets or universal rites, but includes the worship and reclaiming of the divine feminine. Many of its followers also look with reverence to the ultimate persecuted woman in Christian history—the witch.

mobilized massive in-person letter-writing events to unseat the judge who gave convicted rapist Brock Turner an uncommonly short six-month sentence for his crime.

The **Witches of Bushwick** is a crew of visual artists, fashion designers, DJs, and performers of all stripes who see the subversive, transformative power in collaboration. The group began by throwing queer parties for women and has since developed into a creative agency behind multi-media events and a print arts magazine called *The Coven*.

Non-profit activist organization **Lady Parts Justice League** may not seem explicitly witchy, but defines itself as "a coven of hilarious badass feminists who use humor and pop culture to expose the haters fighting against reproductive rights." When asked how the group's aims connect with witchcraft, comedian, co-creator of *The Daily Show,* and founder of LPJL Lizz Winstead told *Slutist*: "Witches brew up good things and dispel evil."

Reclaiming the powerful practice of gathering and crafting by hand, Brooklyn's **Ravenous Craft** is another collective with the structure of a coven. What started as seven women who barely knew one another transformed into a group that meets once a month to cook, share, create, and experiment under a full moon.

Inspired to share their ritual of earth-conscious upcycling and communal connection, this tight-knit crew of creatrixes now offers tutorials and monthly classes on making everything from balms, salves, and candles to tinctures and woven wall hangings.

Their call is to "reconnect with your wild nature" through the process of working harmoniously with the natural world, and they accomplish this in both closed events and those open to the public.

I met three of Ravenous Craft's coven members, Marielle, Mallory, and Erin, in their workshop to discuss the origins of their crafty sisterhood.

What was your first meeting like?

Mallory: The impetus for the first Ravenous dinner was that I knew all these rad women one on one. Growing up, I was always more of a lone wolf (rather, Erin and I were like sister lone wolves), so I figured, let me try joining together some of my favorite babes to see what the fuck happens. And that first night was magical. We made beeswax candles. . . .

Marielle: There were explosions, knife wielding [laughs]. . . .

Mallory: We all got real and crude and vulgar and listened to metal. No conversation topic was off the table. This was long before the witch trend, but Rosemary kept making fun of me because at the time my kitchen had so many dried herbs and jars all over the place, and a cauldron, and she was saying, "I keep feeling like you're gonna take some children and boil them." And we were like, "Yeah! We're like a coven."

Erin: But that's the thing, our boyfriends and whoever else we'd mention that we're having a monthly full moon dinner would say, "Oh are you going to go meet with your witches? Are you meeting with your coven?"

Marielle: Eventually if people would ask though, we'd say, "Don't worry about it. We're having such a good time that we don't need to tell other people about it. It's just for us."

Erin: But then as we learned more about the history and archetype of the witch, we really related to it. The gatherings are for growing and developing and bonding with each other, and it doesn't end up just being about the dinner and the craft. It's about our lives and bringing things to the table and setting intentions and making sure that we are all communicating with one another about things you don't necessarily talk to your significant other or co-workers about.

And you're defying that whole narrative of other women as competition.

Mallory: Because that's a constructed narrative!

Marielle: Yeah, we also admire and acknowledge each other's differences and flaws. A lot of people, especially in girl groups, acknowledge people's flaws—but as a fault. We just see them as a different way of looking at things. There's no jealousy or expectations. We have a very good understanding of the differences among the group and can be better people because we can help each other. It's a positive thing to be able to see things differently.

There's room for everyone.
Erin: As we realized how awesome of a thing this was—it not only helped us as a group but individually—we thought this should be something that everyone should experience. Mallory started an Instagram to document the things we were making. People started saying, "Oh my god I want this for myself" and wanted to join us, but the whole thing is that it's a close-knit personal thing that we want everyone to develop on their own. Right now I'm talking to someone in Portland who's trying to start something similar.

Mallory: Yeah, I mean women gathering in this way is not a new concept. I think it's been silenced for many years with the banishing of the witch and the Satanic Panic, but it's part of our DNA as wild women. It's time for the coven gathering to make a reappearance. I see the Ravenous Craft ethos as a natural thing that feels intuitive and will propagate like wild spores.

Marielle: It's just something we tried and loved it, and we want to share it.

Mallory: Because of the overwhelming positive response, and all the comments from people saying they wanted to join, I figured we would try hosting workshops to give people the tools to start their own covens, and to post craft tutorials and recipes for group meals on the Ravenous Craft website. All of our crafts use natural materials, like recycled elements or foraged items from the park or nature instead of going to Michael's to buy materials that will end up in a landfill. Ultimately, what we're trying to do is promote sisterhood, awareness of the environmental impact our consumer-driven society has had, and develop intuitive and creative prowess.

MUSIC WITCH: SOUND AS SORCERY

The witch has been the mercurial subject of music for centuries. She stars in the diabolical orgy from "Dream of the Night of the Sabbath," the fifth movement of Hector Berlioz's 1830 *Symphonie fantastique*.

She becomes the fearsome hag Baba Yaga in "The Hut on Fowl's Legs" from Modest Mussorgsky's 1874 suite *Pictures at an Exhibition*.

She appears as the beauty with "raven hair and ruby lips" in The Eagles' hit "Witchy Woman" from 1972.

When male musicians create work about the witch, she often serves to elicit fear or arousal. She is a foil for their desires, for their fantasies. She is the mysterious Other.

When the witch herself is positioned as composer, however, the timbre and topic of songs audibly shift to reflect something deeper, tapping into generations of pain and power.

Coven was one of the first bands to openly embrace the aesthetic and practice of witchcraft. Helmed by Jinx Dawson, who hails from a long line of occult practitioners, Coven didn't merely mine America's mid-century occult revival for shock value to enhance its image. The band's 1969 debut album, *Witchcraft Destroys Minds and Reaps Souls*, combines psychedelic rock with esoteric folklore, medieval history, and a Satanic mass. "It was meant to be a scholarly and definitive musical work on witchcraft," Dawson said in an interview with *Confessions of a Pop Culture Addict*.

A few years later, in 1974, one of rock's most reviled women, Yoko Ono, released the funk-driven "Yes, I'm A Witch" as a response to her sexist critics. In a song with personal and political implications and unrepentant feminist messaging, the Japanese artist speaks to generations of female persecution with her straightforward lyrics: "Yes, I'm a witch, I'm a bitch, I don't care what you say," she sings. "My voice is real, my voice is truth, I don't fit in your ways, I'm not gonna die for you."

At the same time, Stevie Nicks was rising to fame with a voice like honey and leather and a penchant for fringe and funereal elegance. She penned Fleetwood Mac's 1975 elegy for a Welsh witch, "Rhiannon," cementing her place as rock music's favorite sorceress—a role she would later play up in the 2013 witch TV drama *American Horror Story: Coven*.

"A long, long time ago I decided I was going to have a kind of mystical presence," Nicks revealed in *Interview*, "so I made my clothes, my boots, my hair, and my whole being go with that. But it wasn't something I just made up at that point. It's the way I've always been. I've always believed in good witches—not bad witches—and fairies and angels."

These pioneering women allied themselves with witches and witchcraft in a time when doing so was dangerous, and could even threaten their creative careers. Their breed continues in a new generation of musicians donning the witch's symphonic shroud.

Throwing open two gilded doors to release a prophetic tidal rush down the stairs, Beyoncé pauses, arms outstretched, in the shape of a cross. The camera focuses in on her bare feet. She strides ahead, golden dress undulating like seaweed, water splashing around her ankles. Once back on dry land, with curls bouncing behind her, she's handed a baseball bat to exact her woman-scorned vengeance on the cars that line the street.

The witch is back.

Like nearly everything the artist releases, Beyoncé's headline-stealing 2016 visual album, *Lemonade*, has been scoured for symbolism, lauded for elevating black femininity, and criticized for promoting consumer capitalism. It also alludes both visually and lyrically to a variety of spiritual practices such as the Yoruba religion, Ifá, Santería, Candomble, and Voodoo. *Lemonade* was called "the epitome of black girl magic" in *The Establishment*, and Beyoncé was described as having "modeled herself into a witch—of the healing variety—during a time when black women are in need of positive reinforcement, deep healing and transformation" in *Billboard*.

Practicing witches were the first to spot the water flowing beneath Beyoncé's golden dress as a reference to Oshun, the Yoruba goddess of water, femininity, and sensuality from an Afro-Latinx spiritual tradition that spans continents and cultures. During the visual accompaniment to the song "6 Inch," Beyoncé channels yet another iteration of Oshun. Electrified in red light in the back of a limousine, she sings, "She loves the grind," while giving eyes to men on the street beneath a broad-brimmed hat. In this moment, some saw the Voodoo lwa Erzulie*, who stokes passions and doesn't trifle with monogamy. As *JuJuMama* asked: Has the queen of pop gone polyamorous? Only time will tell.

Although Beyoncé herself has never publicly claimed to be a witch—and was even accused by some witches of appropriating witch imagery as a marketing ploy—other female musicians have become more and more explicit about their witchcraft practice in the past decade.

In 2015, rapper Azealia Banks announced her witch identity to the world on Twitter, saying: "I'm really a witch. . . . The most magical people are the ones who have to deal with

---

* Lwa or loa are a diverse coterie of spirits in the Voodoo pantheon.

oppression, because the non-magical are jealous." Banks came out of the broom closet more publicly than any witch before her, perhaps revealing an increasing acceptance of witch-identified women—at least when they happen to be famous musicians.

Christiana Key, a practicing witch and musician, has incorporated participatory rituals into her performances as Delphic Oracle for over five years. To celebrate pagan holidays such as Ostara and Walpurgisnacht or to transform a regular night into something sacred, Key organizes immersive experiences with fire, incense, dancers, and hand-crafted offerings. Her concerts are a space for connection, for letting go, and for receiving guidance. She encourages her audience to contend with their own demons as they take in her hypnotic soprano incantations set to violin and synthesizers.

"It is my purpose, every performance, to have the audience lose ego, even for a moment; to absorb everything coming at their senses without a filter, without fear," Key told *Slutist* in 2013.

"The myths, rituals, and other details used during Delphic Oracle performances are already embedded into our ancestral makeup. It is my responsibility to bring them out and emblazon them in the forefront of our hearts and minds."

Ghanaian artist Azizaa is a self-identified witch who makes "Voodoo music." Her 2015 video for "Black Magic Woman" is a celebration of transgressive female power and alludes to a lineage of oppressive Christian patriarchy. It begins with men in missionary garb proselytizing aggressively to a woman, eventually groping her as she tries to escape their clutches. At the next cut, Azizaa towers above them in triple horned braids. "I see through your visions," she intones, and pounds a staff on the forest ground as the men cower with Bibles in hand.

In an interview with *The Fader*, Azizaa expressed her opposition to destructive Christian dogma that dominates her West African country. "In Ghana, most people believe in following the crowd just to stay alive, not to be scrutinized," she said. "There is stigma attached to vodou, so Christianity is a very safe choice. But deep down, in their souls, hearts and minds, they can't fight or ignore the voice that tells them to go back to their roots."

In contrast with these artists, Hether Fortune is a witch and musician who does not explicitly share her spiritual identity through her music or live shows. Although her band, Wax Idols, is informed by her personal practice, Fortune is bewitching because of her songwriting and the way she moves her body, wields her guitar, and engages with her audience.

"I'm definitely not the kind of artist who is like, 'I'm a witch and I make witch music,'" she told *Noisey.* "I'm a pop writer. It doesn't correlate in a very obvious way. But what I am worked out in a lot of ways through music and the process of writing and performing. It's extremely ritualistic for me."

Music boasts a bevy of self-identified witches, making it a haven for practitioners to both explicitly and implicitly enact their sonic sorcery. Using language, repetition, visuals, and the voice in hypnotic ways, these witches are spellcasting every time they take the stage—and every time we hit play. As in art, film, and literature, the witch's popularity continues to transcend genre and gender. But although the witch has undoubtedly been the fertile subject of music for centuries, now more than ever she is its formidable creatrix, too.

HEX SELLS: FEMINISM, CAPITALISM & THE WITCH

Thanks to the burgeoning popularity of witches, you, too, can adorn yourself in the dark, seductive trappings of sorcery. Like punk, many once marginalized movements are now fodder for the marketplace. As the cultural sphere is gobbled up by the consumer sphere at warp speed, American hypercapitalism has rendered rebellion an act often performed via spending habits. Although it may be in style to sport the phrase "Witch, Please" on your beanie or to wear a velvet hooded cape in a bid to cloak yourself in occult feminine power, consumers may also be supporting sweatshops overseas that treat female garment workers like slaves or enabling practices that pollute the environment in the process.

To explore the intersection between witches, feminism, and capitalism—and to find out what is being sold to a public with an appetite for all things occult—I visited an Urban Outfitters in Santa Monica, California, a teeming tourist destination.

With more than two hundred stores in the US, Canada, and Europe, Urban Outfitters is, according to its website, a "lifestyle retailer dedicated to inspiring customers through a unique combination of product, creativity and cultural understanding." The last part of this description is a bit hypocritical, however. Urban Outfitters has notoriously gotten into hot water for stealing designs from independent artists and for peddling questionable items such as striped shirts with pink triangles akin to what the Nazis forced gay prisoners to wear, undergarments named the "Navajo Hipster Panty," and shirts with a color option called "Obama/Black."

Here is a small sampling of the witchy items I found at Urban Outfitters:

"Clear Mind" spray by Little Moon Essentials (described as "a uniquely therapeutic aromatherapy mist")

"Moonlight Bath Bag" by House of Intuition (described as an herbal bath with "a potent influence on the mind and spirit creating a magical synergy")

Holy Basil + Rose Sacred Smudge by Plantfolk (described as an herbal incense blend to burn "mindfully" to release unwanted energies and "purify the air")

Golden Universal Tarot decks by Roberto De Angelis

Food Fortunes by Josh Lafayette (described as a mystical set of cards that answer the ancient mystery: "What's for dinner tonight")

Untold quantities of black, fringed, witch-adjacent clothing

Perusing the store, I found it ironic that witch merch is so in vogue, given that the archetypal witch can be viewed as an early modern threat to mercantilism. As Marxist feminist scholar Silvia Federici argues, the witch is "the embodiment of a world of female subjects that capitalism had to destroy" in order for the reigning economic order to triumph. And yet, because mainstream economic, religious, medicinal, cultural, and political structures arguably don't offer much in the way of affordable and effective self-care, the trend of witchy herbs and potions being sold at corporate retailers can also be viewed as an answer to the primal need to re-connect with our wild natures and heal ourselves.

Separating what is commodified rebellion and what is a genuine attempt at spreading alternative ideologies or practices is exceedingly difficult. At first glance, it was unclear to me which products were produced with some modicum of authenticity by independent small businesses and merely distributed by Urban Outfitters, and which were directly produced by the company. I wondered what kind of production and distribution practices must be in place for aesthetic empowerment to transcend the surface level and have real impact. Because the corporate world will always look to co-opt subcultures for profit, it's valuable to explore how this process can both help and hinder those who are part of these subcultures.

In 1993, writer and activist Pat Califia wrote about his feelings regarding Madonna's appropriation of BDSM culture for her coffee-table book *Sex*. In an essay for fetish magazine *Skin Two*, he described how difficult it was to see the pop star cashing in on inauthentic portrayals of kink when members of his community were still being marginalized and even prosecuted for their consensual practices.

"I feel deeply ambivalent about somebody who has not paid her dues using my community as a series of bizarre backdrops for a photoshoot," he explained.

In 2016, famed pandrogynous musician and occultist Genesis Breyer P-Orridge told *Dazed* magazine that the trend of "gender free" fashion is profiting off the trans community, which faces extreme levels of violence and state-sanctioned persecution.

"What's been co-opted is the politics of identity," s/he said, "and it has been trivialized into one season's fashion and that's a dangerous way of reducing the importance of the real issues. And that's something that the corporate world does very well. They always co-opt and even coerce new radical ideas that express the underground, the street culture, and they do it very deliberately because they realized a very long time ago that if they reduce it and co-opt it, it loses its power to change anything."

Urban Outfitters is undoubtedly cashing in on witchcraft,

and tapping into the spiritual industrial complex to sell spooky swag. The occult practices it capitalizes on might once have gotten you killed were you caught observing them openly, and might still be cause for ostracism, losing a job, or losing custody of your children in certain communities today.

However, what stores like Urban Outfitters—and every mall goth's favorite, Hot Topic—offer is unprecedented access to subcultures often out of reach for young people. Those in rural areas without a local witch shop or knowledge about the occultic side of the internet can be introduced to an entire subculture through these stores. Perhaps they will pick up a tarot deck first as a gag gift, and then look further into the ancient practice of divination, and maybe even learn about the feminist history of Pamela Coleman Smith, a member of British occult society the Hermetic Order of the Golden Dawn, who is responsible for creating the iconic images on the ubiquitous Rider-Waite deck.

Where democratic dissemination ends and exploitation begins is tricky territory.

The same issues are at play within contemporary feminism. When is marketing feminist products a gateway to radical, life-changing ideas, and when is it merely watering down and co-opting a movement for corporate gain? *Bitch Media* co-founder Andi Zeisler's *We Were Feminists Once: From Riot Grrrl to CoverGirl, the Buying and Selling of a Political Movement* unpacks this complex issue.

Zeisler first looks into the ways feminism has driven corporate commerce, opening her book with a ludicrous advertisement using the Seneca Falls Convention to sell women Platinum MasterCards. Women have always been a target consumer demographic, she explains, even before "the f-word" rose to prominence. In years past, companies chased after women to buy Maidenform bras and Virginia Slims cigarettes using language that embodied feminine freedom, and now it's Dove Body Wash. The common denominator? Selling liberation through lifestyle goods.

Zeisler writes: "The narrative that feminism has succeeded

because it's all over the internet, because it's a marketing buzz-word, because there's a handful of famous people happy to serve as its icons is as wrongheaded as the notion that feminism suc-ceeded when (white) women got the vote or when the first fe-male CEO stepped a sensible shoe into her spacious office."

This misguided perspective is what some have called "Lean In Feminism," named after Facebook COO Sheryl Sandberg's book about corporate women breaking the glass ceiling: *Lean In: Women, Work, and the Will to Lead.*

In a 2013 piece for *The Feminist Wire*, bell hooks takes Sandberg's feminist philosophy to task. "Sandberg's definition of feminism begins and ends with the notion that it's all about gender equality within the existing social system," hooks writes. "From this perspective, the structures of imperialist white su-premacist capitalist patriarchy need not be challenged. And she makes it seem that privileged white men will eagerly choose to extend the benefits of corporate capitalism to white women who have the courage to 'lean in.'"

So if feminism has a capitalism problem, as hooks—and many others—suggest, how does this impact our shopping habits?

Sometimes it takes a little digging to know exactly where your clothes are coming from. Brands waving the flag for fem-inism from Beyoncé's Ivy Park line to "This Is What a Feminist Looks Like" T-shirts produced by *Elle* and the Fawcett Society have come under scrutiny in recent years for their alleged ties to sweatshops. The frequently horrific conditions of the gar-ment industry overseas are not only a human rights issue, but a feminist issue tied into capitalist production, sex work, and sexual autonomy.

In countries such as Cambodia, Haiti, and India, anti-sex-trafficking narratives promoted by certain prominent fem-inists and NGOs in the United States end up criminalizing and endangering sex workers who consensually work in the sex in-dustry, which forces them into the frequently harsher and more dangerous conditions of the garment industry. Anne Elizabeth

Moore and The Ladydrawers' comic exposé *Threadbare: Clothes, Sex and Trafficking* analyzes this cycle of profiteering, production, and consumption driven by the fashion market.

In a world where women are vying for their right to make a living how they individually see fit, it's dangerous to assume that sex work is more degrading than factory work, Moore asserts. "Workers at every stage of apparel production and distribution . . . suffer low wages, sexual and gender-based harassment, and hostile work environments ranging from insufficient health care to worker shootings," she elaborates.

These links reveal how shopping at corporate retailers can directly contribute to the further marginalization of women— and movements you respect. There is, however, an alternative.

Many feminists and witch-identified creators offer their ethically made wares through Etsy, Big Cartel, and independently owned and run sites and shops across the country. Some even donate a portion of their proceeds to non-profits that seek to improve the lives of women the world over. Of course, not everyone has the education or privilege to actively *buy*cott problematic products or research the ways corporate retailers build their brands on exploitation—so buyer beware. As hex continues to sell, and feminism remains in style, cultural capital often translates to consumer capitalism, which ultimately advocates for the rights of no one.

TECH WITCH: ONLINE ACTIVISM & THE DIGITAL MYSTIC

"We can revolutionize the world we were born into
by using the witchcraft skills of compassion, genius,
insight, intuition, and talent."

—Dame Darcy

Drawn together by the labyrinthine networks that link the like-minded, "generation witch" is a product of contemporary technology. Creating community has become ritualized in new ways: the selfie, the hashtag, the snap, the swipe. As the wireless world blurs IRL and URL, and with it our so-called "real selves" and online personas, we have the opportunity to connect with more people than ever before.

During the early days of the internet, some predicted the digital sphere would become a utopia where equality flourished, and identity categories dissolved. Maria Fernandez writes in *Domain Errors!: Cyberfeminist Practice*, "Electronic media theorists and commercial entities alike maintain that 'differences' of gender, race and class are nonexistent in the internet due to the disembodied nature of electronic communication."

At the time, there were also cyberfeminists who saw the flaws in this perspective. Beth Kolko et al. offer a contrasting viewpoint in *Race in Cyberspace*. "Cyberspace has been construed as something that exists in binary opposition to 'the real world,'" they write, "but when it comes to questions of power, politics and structural relations, cyberspace is as real as it gets."

Almost two decades later, identity politics have both blossomed and festered in cyberspace—and people from marginalized groups face the highest levels of harassment online. Black and Latinx people are more likely to be harassed online than white people; every ten seconds someone calls a woman a "slut" or a "whore" on Twitter; 25 percent of women between the ages of eighteen and twenty-four have reported being sexually harassed online; and 26 percent of women in that age group have been stalked online, too. In spite of (or because of) this fact, those from racialized and gendered spaces have often been able to make their voices heard above the digital din.

According to 2015 data from Pew Research on social media demographics, 28 percent of black and Hispanic internet users are on Twitter, compared with 20 percent of white users. Digital activism on Twitter is led by people of color. Hashtags like #BlackLivesMatter, #SayHerName, #SolidarityIsForWhite-Women, and #BlackGirlMagic advocate to raise awareness about systemic racial inequality, memorialize murdered black women and girls, reveal racial divisions amongst feminists, and celebrate the beauty and accomplishments of black women, respectively.

These hashtags were coined, championed, and transformed into real world action because of Black Twitter.

When it comes to gender-driven politics online, the "Feminist internet" takes charge—although Black Twitter overlaps with this arm of internet activism and often leads the way there as well.

In the same abovementioned Pew demographic research, women were found to outnumber men on nearly every social media platform but Twitter. #RapeCultureIsWhen, #FreeTheNipple, #MasculinitySoFragile, and #EffYourBeautyStandards are all examples of women driving the discussion online toward rape culture, gender bias and body positivity, toxic masculinity, and overcoming oppressive beauty standards.

Online spaces continue to foster feminist community and provide an invaluable platform for feminist politics.

As sex-positive feminist activist Feminista Jones wrote in *Salon*: "140 characters can be all it takes to spark a movement."

Millennials are the first native digital generation to have grown up online, and because the internet is divested from nature—from sunrise and sunset and the seasons to the waxing and waning moon—some have responded with increased investment in the earth. As a new wave of interest in the witch rises, information on nature-based practices is proliferating. There are social media hubs where you can learn how to use ritual to heal from trauma, how to use sex magic to achieve desired goals, and how to harness the power of natural objects for a variety of purposes. Many of these witchcraft practices are rooted in ancient—and even historically secretive—traditions, but are now available to the masses in digital grimoires.

There is a uniquely twenty-first-century kind of magic, however, that straddles the physical and virtual worlds and could not exist offline.

Digital artist Molly Soda's interactive "Virtual Spellbook" is one space that offers spells to bless a new cellphone, banish an internet troll, or prevent yourself from checking an ex-lover's social media account. Each magical recipe requires working in both analog and digital, with objects and ideas, whether speaking aloud or typing online, imagining the ephemeral or engaging with the earth.

One step further removed from the physical world is writer and witch Tarin Towers' emoji spells. In a 2015 article for *Broadly*, Towers explains how to use the variety of colorful ideograms at our disposal in magical ways. She outlines how to call in prosperity, shield yourself from negative influences, or unbind yourself from a lover after a breakup using only your desires and your smartphone. These spells can be enacted by

messaging yourself with a string of emoji sent in a particular order, texting them to a friend, or even posting a screencapture to Instagram.

Witchcraft is not merely a solitary practice, so when witches take these digital tools and join together, the results can be powerful. Collective spellcasting happened with increased frequency over the past few years. As activists organized online in the name of social justice, thousands of self-identified witches, mystics, occultists, and intuitives simultaneously connected through social media to hex and heal, as they set their sights on fighting racism, sexism, xenophobia, homophobia, and transphobia through any means necessary.

Shortly after Trump's inauguration, a group called the Yerbamala Collective published dozens of anti-fascist poems online to "destroy fascism with poetic witchcraft." They instructed allies to disseminate their "Our Vendetta: Witches Vs Fascists" writings widely, to send a message across state and community lines. "If the broom/ fits witch it/ is time to/ ride it/ act up/ resist," decreed one terse, compelling poem.

In an article for *The Hoodwitch*, queer astrologer and witch Jaliessa Sipress expressed what it means to practice witchcraft in the age of Trump. His presidency is "a mere practice in veil-lifting," she wrote, "another opportunity to practice seeing in the dark, and revealing our political and social climate for what it really is only makes our work that much more important."

While attempting to survive in and resist an administration that supports inhumane, discriminatory policies, disregards objective reality, and promotes "alternative facts," many witches are uniting in the physical and digital realms against the rise of a new Christian theocracy. This fight is on the internet as much as it is on the ground, against the fake news stories spewing distortions and inflammatory lies meant to stoke fears of a demonized Other—much like *The Malleus Maleficarum* and similar tracts did in the early modern era.

Collective spellcasting need not only be thought of in spiritual terms, as it functions similarly to the way people collectively rally behind a hashtag to inspire media coverage, drive real world protest, influence representatives, and, eventually, enact laws and national change. If language can be a spell, and repetition a method to transform intent into action, harnessing the collective consciousness through viral activist campaigns is one way witches are using their magic to fight back against oppression.

THE LEGACY OF THE WITCH

"Unruly women are always witches, no matter what century we're in."

—Roxane Gay

Witchcraft is embedded into the landscape of modern-day Salem, Massachusetts. A stark, blood-red line cuts through the town to lead visitors across the Salem Heritage Trail. It's not a strange sight to see someone in seventeenth-century Puritan dress scurrying down an alleyway, buckle shoes clicking on asphalt.

Occult shops pepper the cheerful streets selling books, herbs, crystals, oils, and handmade corn husk poppets. Novelty shops offer spooky tchotchkes in the form of "Girls Night Out" tees printed with witches in a flying V, or bumper stickers that read "My other car is a broom." There are year-round tours that delve into witch trials history, pilgrim ghost stories, and contemporary witchcraft. Multiple museums boast the word "witch" in the title, and each offers a slightly different take on what exactly happened in 1692.

The city's macabre history is inescapable.

As with any tourist destination, there are some places that seem bent on making a buck. These are the tackier establishments, making light of the brutality or merely reveling in its lurid details. But these parts of Salem are easy to see through. When you look closer, there are many who are serious about learning from the legacy of the witch and passing on that knowledge to any visitor who will listen.

Following in the footsteps of all those who make the pilgrimage to Salem with their ghoulfriends looking for witchy respite, I signed up for a walking tour led by a practicing local witch. A Christian couple from West Virginia, an eight-year-old boy wearing plastic fangs, and a trio of po-faced goth teens were just some of the folks who took part. It was a motley crew, to say the least.

After joining together in a nondenominational pagan ritual where the group invoked the power of nature or the deity of our choosing for protection, we headed toward the cemetery. Next to the grassy, shaded burial ground marked with the aging graves of Salem notables is the Salem Witch Trials Memorial. A protruding stone slab is dedicated to each victim, listing their names and how they died. As you enter the area, you're likely to step across a thin strip of stone chiseled with the incomplete last words of convicted "witches." It's so subtle you could easily miss it. The guide points out how the pleas of these innocent dead would be forever trampled by oblivious visitors walking through. The symbolism is undeniable.

As we traversed the monument and the cemetery, our witch guide discussed contemporary witchcraft practices and the persecution of witches over the centuries. She spoke about the archetypal goddess triad—maiden, mother, and crone—and how contemporary feminist and witchcraft scholars are reframing these stages for a more expansive and inclusive take on womanhood. All the while she hammered home again and again how uninformed our cultural image of the witch is.

Witches are not servants of the Devil, she said, and in fact, witches can follow any religion and still practice witchcraft. Witches do not all dress in flowing robes (although, natch, it's fun to do). Witches do not eat babies—but they do drink Dunkin Donuts coffee. Witches, too, run on Dunkin, she joked.

Witches! They're just like us.

With such an accessible, down-to-earth explanation of witchcraft and witch history, one can only assume those who entered the tour filled with pejorative propaganda about witches would abandon much of it by the end.

And I hope you'll leave this primer in similar fashion.

After my childhood obsession with Maleficent metamorphosed into a serious exploration of witches and feminism, my academic involvement made me privy to a whole new generation of witch hunts. Whenever class discussions turn personal—as they often do when discussing gender issues—it isn't uncommon for a young woman to detail an experience in her religious or conservative upbringing where her anatomy was not only destiny, but devilry. Of the dozens of students I've taught over the years, there are more than a few who have been deemed demonic and literally called "witches" in ways that would make *The Malleus Maleficarum* author Heinrich Kramer grin in his putrid grave. The more it happens, the less I respond, nonplussed.

These are not tales plucked from the dusty annals of history. These are the lived experiences of college students in contemporary America, where the specter of the witch still haunts women to this day. Although the witch-hunting era did officially end, it did not end all witch hunts, nor did it end the practice of women being scapegoated for society's ills.

By the eighteenth century, witch hysteria began to wane in Europe and America. A combination of Enlightenment ideals and modern science gaining prominence helped to shift cultural focus away from sorcery as the sole source of death, disaster, and misfortune. Great Britain's Witchcraft Act of 1735 made it illegal for anyone to claim they were magical or to accuse someone of practicing witchcraft, and similar laws across the European continent were drafted to reflect this change in attitudes.

The status of women began to shift after the witch-hunting era, too. The same scientific and Enlightenment advancements that helped put an end to the witch hunts also helped dispel a few damning demonological myths about women and female sexuality. However, sexism remained endemic, and misogyny merely became medicalized.

In the nineteenth century, unruly women were no longer witches in need of purification by fire, but hysterics, forced to undergo barbarous treatments deemed cutting edge by medical professionals at the time. Like witchcraft before it, hysteria (aka "womb disease") was a catch-all diagnosis that punished anxious, depressed, wayward, or highly sexual women, and contrary to popular belief, a solo date with a dildo was the least invasive of its prescribed "cures."

In the twentieth century, the feminist movement took great strides to improve the legal and social position of women. But, as ever, women still face sexist violence and still fight for bodily autonomy and access to reproductive health care today—and there is no shortage of politicians and religious leaders with opinions on how women should behave.

Outside the Western bubble, however, women are currently accused of witchcraft in shocking numbers.

Women deemed witches for decades have been banished to "witch camps" in Ghana, where a belief in witchcraft persists amongst the population. Two thousand people accused of witchcraft have been murdered in Northeast India over the last fifteen years—the majority women—and an estimated six hundred elderly women were killed in 2011 because they were suspected of practicing witchcraft in Tanzania.

In 2015, a graphic video uploaded by citizens in Papua New Guinea showed four women accused of witchcraft stripped naked and burned alive. According to some tribal beliefs, the womb houses evil spirits, and women are most often thought to be witches after unexplained deaths or monetary and property conflicts arise in their communities. Estimates by the United Nations list the numbers of witch executions at around two hundred a year, and until 2013, murdering a witch in self-defense was enshrined in the country's constitution.

Witch hunting in the very literal sense occurs with alarming frequency, but there are those who fight back to help persecuted women in need. Amnesty International created the Women Not Witches outreach program, and local activists on the frontlines have formed grassroots groups to tackle witch hunts and misogyny in their individual countries.

For the past fifteen years, Birubala Rabha has been one of these crusaders in the northern Indian state of Assam. In a place where women are still brutalized for being suspected witches, she campaigns tirelessly to educate local communities and governments about the error in their beliefs. According to an article in BBC News, her efforts have saved dozens of women's lives, and even helped inspire a 2015 anti-witch-hunting law.

"They will always find new reasons to brand women as witches," Rabha said to a gathering of women in Assam. "But don't be scared, challenge the offenders and report them to the police. This battle is not going to end anytime soon."

Those accused of witchcraft, witch-identified women, and scholars are most intimate with the pain and suffering women accused of witchcraft have endured throughout history. For the rest, the witch remains a costume, a grade school social studies project, the star of their favorite movie, or a haunted hag to shudder over once a year when the press shines a light on the occult.

Yet millennial women's growing interest in the witch—and, in particular, the renewed feminist association with the witch— might signal something deeper. Could there be another element that connects us to the witch's lineage?

Since the early modern era, countless people have been accused of witchcraft around the world. The families of these supposed witches often saw their loved ones tortured, raped, hanged, burned, and drowned in state-sponsored exterminations for their supposed crimes. But some accused witches survived their trials to be found not guilty.

To survive suffering can sometimes mean to swallow it whole, transmitting the experience to a cellular level. New scientific evidence suggests that one organism's trauma can be passed on genetically to future generations.

In 2013, researchers at Emory University in Atlanta gave male mice an electric shock, accompanied by the scent of cherry blossoms. Every time they were subjected to the odor, they were zapped. Eventually, the mere scent of cherry blossom resulted in the mice cowering in fear.

In what scientists called "epigenetic inheritance," the next generation of mice, who had never been exposed to the electric shock or even a whiff of cherry blossom, exhibited a fear response when they came in contact with the scent.

Scientists discovered these offspring had more brain space dedicated to the receptor that allowed them to detect the odor of cherry blossoms, and they reacted to much lower levels. They also found that female mice could pass along the same generational memory, manifested in a survival mechanism.

Although the idea of physically manifesting memories sounds like quackery to some—and many scientists caution against making broad-brush assumptions about the epigenetic phenomenon—there are numerous human examples that reflect this mouse-tested theory.

Rachel Yehuda is a researcher in the growing field of epigenetics, and has studied the effects of mass trauma on the offspring of survivors. Her work was discussed in *Scientific American* in an article detailing the ways descendants of Holocaust survivors have "different stress hormone profiles than their peers," including lower levels of cortisol, which helps the human body deal with stress.

The offspring of Holocaust survivors are less equipped than their parents were to deal with stress. In effect, the trauma their ancestors faced has compromised their coping mechanisms. Unlike mice, who adapted positively to their ancestors' trauma, these humans did not.

The research is preliminary, but telling.

"If you are looking for it all to be logical and fall into place perfectly, it isn't going to yet," Yehuda explains. "We are just at the beginning of understanding this."

Epigenetic studies have also explored intergenerational trauma in Native American populations, and in those who have survived sexual abuse. Sociologist Dr. Daron T. Smith has written about the effects of intergenerational trauma on the African American descendants of slaves.

"The science of epigenetics is unlocking significant clues as to how racial discrimination can induce changes to the expression of certain genes linked to biological development and the existence of disease," he wrote in *The Huffington Post*. "These epigenetic changes can linger for a lifetime and can potentially be transmitted to offspring."

In response to thousands of women harassed, tortured, or murdered for supposedly practicing witchcraft, is it possible that their relatives, too, retain a trace of this trauma?

Feminist author Starhawk theorizes that the brutal history of witch hunting "remains with us today as a wound in the collective psyche." Following epigenetic theory, could this trauma have snaked its way into an accused witch descendant's DNA?

How many of us are the granddaughters of the witches they could not burn?

To reframe Carol F. Karlsen's statement in *The Devil in the Shape of a Woman*, the history of the witch is primarily a history of women. Whether in art, film, music, fashion, literature, technology, religion, pop culture, or politics, the witch is an enduring symbol of liberation and oppression, and an icon of sexual and intellectual freedom.

The advent of feminism has provided many women the human rights they have lacked and craved for centuries, but many still suffer under misogyny's yoke. There is much work required to challenge the sexist discourse that denigrates consensual female sexual pleasure and prevents female bodily autonomy from being fully realized.

The arduous journey toward gender equality continues,

and when women navigate this mercurial topography, the witch stands out as a beacon in black. In the face of oppression, the witch reminds us what we can and have overcome, and illuminates the path to power beyond patriarchy. As we undress the legacy of the witch to reveal her potent history, we may in the process uncover something marrow-deep within our ourselves.

WHAT IS A WITCH? SURVEY

I surveyed fifty people through Twitter and Facebook, asking them what the word "witch" means to them. These are a selection of the responses:

Lee, 21: A magic-user but with definite connotations of queerness.

Christy, 68: A woman with magical powers.

Lindsey, 29: A female that practices Wicca or otherwise believes in a similar way of relating with the natural world.

Anne, 53: Emotionally, I think of someone who is evil.

Kathleen, 67. A powerful woman who uses her intuition and personal power for good or bad.

Beck, 19: People who harness the energies of the world to do right. Put good karma out. Closely related to the Wiccan religion in practice and rhetoric.

Samantha, 23: A female with magical talents or gifts. It's really a mixture of Hermione Granger and the coven season of *American Horror Story*.

Sarah, 29: Someone who performs magick, and may or may not have a relationship with the Gods.

Cindy, 44: A woman with supernatural powers and a command of "natural" magic.

Haley, 27: Long-haired pagan lesbians with bohemian fashion sense.

Alicia, 40: Wise and wizened woman, usually self-reliant, often ostracized until people need something from her. Or the idea of the nature goddess, who has a relationship with nature and the wild world around her. Again, she's her own woman.

Margaret, 50: I grew up in a time of *Bewitched* reruns. Witches were cute blondes married to regular people trying to keep their powers under control.

Ed, 30: Empowered female.

Mindy, 32: Change maker.

Whitney, 29: A magical woman.

Jamey, 39: Mystical, dark, femme.

Jack, 25: Brujería. Oyá. Spirituality. The Caribbean. It also means the appropriation and exploitation of indigenous belief systems by white people who killed us for our culture only to make it "trendy" later.

Bill, 44: One who is wise in the "old ways." One who not just studies but actually practices them as well. A "Witch" is one with the Natural World and uses natural forces daily.

Kim, 28: An archaic term for a magical, evil, or otherwise misunderstood but demonstrably powerful woman; a healer; a feminist; a trendy Etsy skull ring collector; a bitch with skills.

Odana, 25: It's a word used to demonize power, opinion, and faculty within women.

Marley, 34: A woman with power. I think of crones in black capes and pointy hats, but also I think of women who have power, any power. To the patriarchy, a woman with any power

(political, physical, mental, influential) doesn't deserve it
or couldn't have earned it. It must be some kind of magic.
. . .Witches are healers, they're wise, they have special knowledge, they're scary because they're different. But most of all,
witches are women who won't conform to the stereotypical
idea of what a woman should be. Witches are the matriarchy
and that's scary. Too fucking bad, men.

Vanessa, 36: A witch is the opposite of a victim.

Kelsey, 29: Any person who employs rituals or practices to seek
an end, whether that means magic, meditation, a curse, etc.

Katrina, 26: A secular, spiritually empowered woman.

Maheen, 33: Wisdom, courage, peace, beauty, nature, and love.
To be a witch is not only a journey of self-discovery, but it also
binds you to nature and to the sanctity of it. Being a witch is
powerful and is something one must follow through for the
rest of their life to really understand it and to appreciate its
history given the modern world we live in. The witch is an
evolving character and she is sought after by those who do not
have the capacity or the gift to fully submerge themselves in
the craft.

Aimeric, 29: Someone living at the crossroad between worlds.

Sonia, 35: Powerful being, healer. One who is connected to
the spirit world and the earth and uses those connections via
magic to create their present.

Natalie, 39: Honestly, my first instinct is the classic Hallow-
een-style witch. Green and warty with a pointy hat, striped
stockings and a cat. It also, unfortunately, usually has a negative connotation depending on the usage. Like, if I were to
hear someone call someone a "witch," I would assume it to not
be a good thing.

Mathieu, 21: Someone wielding great power and confidence,
generally feminine.

Devon, 32: A femme that tinkers with reality. I know all the old etymologies and that, but to me it means someone who hones personal discipline in a certain way to achieve psychic ends.

INTERVIEW WITH A WITCH

How did you first to come into your witch identity?
I grew up in New England, not too far from Salem, Massachusetts, where my parents met. It's just part of the culture in New England. I think the first time I started trying to do magic, I was nine years old and I had my first coven with three other girls. We were really obsessed with telepathy and spent a lot of time getting any witchy books we could find out of the library. By the time I was in junior high, I was wearing all black, and I found it very protective for people to think that I could curse them or mess with them because I got a lot of harassment for just being weird, and all the typical teenage bullshit. Because I was near Salem, I was fascinated with Laurie Cabot and Wicca. That spoke to me the most, but I feel that if I have a religion, it is Nature. I think that studying occult and esoteric subjects is about looking for answers to try to make sense of all the experiences I had as a child and throughout my life. For me, magic is validating your own extrasensory perceptions and being free in your mind. —Darcey Leonard

It kind of started when I was young. Being a closeted queer trans Latina, I often felt really weird and different and bad, and I didn't really know why. I felt like everyone else was looking at me and judging me and thinking I was evil. When I finally came out in my twenties, I decided to reclaim those feelings of alienation and weirdness and wrongness that I had felt my entire life. I was remaking my spirituality and my aesthetic and my attitude, and I decided to embrace all the things that make me witchy. My family comes from a long line of Mexican Catholics, so I started to incorporate La Virgen de Guadalupe and Santa Muerte into my practice. I've always used candles for prayer, so I started doing candle magic. Now that I was an out trans woman, people openly started treating me like an outsider and strange creature, so I doubled down on that. If I'm a witch, I get power from being weird and from being hated by others. If I'm a witch, no one can tell me I'm wrong for being different. I'm telling them I'm different, and I'm telling them that makes me strong. —**Mey Rude**

The first person to ever tell me calmly that I was a witch was a roommate I had in San Francisco when I was twenty or twenty-one. He and I had been living together for only a few months but had become incredibly close through a series of nights spent listening to The Smiths and complaining about people while chain smoking in the kitchen. He was an artist in his thirties, working at a porn shop in the Castro to pay his way through design school, and also happened to be a descendent of a long line of New Orleans witches and healers. I think I always knew I was a witch, but my time spent with him allowed me to verbally and specifically identify myself as such. He simply called it as it was, and my life made a lot more sense after that. I learned a lot from him about color work, herbs, the power of words and numbers, etc. When I started using applied ritual methods to whatever natural witch abilities I'd always had, things started opening up a lot more for me. My creativity started blossoming at a really accelerated rate, I began feeling more comfortable and confident in my body, and I started learning how to value myself and my mind in new ways that absolutely changed my life. I realized that I already had a tremendous amount of power inside of me and that I could use that power to protect myself, to protect other people, and to have more control over my own life. Witchcraft isn't about superstitions and meddling in the lives of others. It's about fully tapping into personal power through a connection to and awareness of the world around you. Life has been much more manageable since I came into acceptance of who and what I am, even if it does still suck being in this body on this planet from time to time. —**Hether Fortune**

As a young, gender-nonconforming queer person, I didn't know exactly what made me feel that "different" feeling most queer people recall having as a child. The best way for me to put that "different" feeling into words was calling myself a witch. I didn't know what it meant outside of what witches were in movies, but they were always some sort of outcast, so I felt like I could relate. I also didn't know I was gay, and it took me over twenty years to feel like I had even the slightest idea of how gender made sense to me. In time, I figured all that stuff out, but identifying as a witch first let me feel like being different was a good thing even when maybe it wasn't ideal. (Children can be cruel.) Also, witches always looked cool as fuck in movies and books, so wearing all black and trying to look like a witch just made me grow a good taste in clothing and styling. —**Severely Mame**

Growing up in New Orleans, I was exposed to magic and "witchy" things much earlier than most. I remember being four or five years old with my parents and visiting some relatives in the French Quarter and just feeling something extra in the air that I couldn't' describe. The older I got, the stronger this feeling was and the more fascinated I became with the history of NOLA. I started with the ghost and vampire stories and those led to the stories of Marie Laveau, the woman who supposedly is still so connected to NOLA that even in death she protects it. When I was in high school, I had the good fortune of meeting a Voodoo priest named John T, who I would remain friends with until his passing twenty years later. He and my studies brought me to incorporating Voodoo as a practice, and I built my first altar at the age of fifteen. (In 1995 this was not something that my parents took lightly.) I learned young that not everyone was ready to accept me being a witch, so I took from Voodoo and masked my practice in Christianity until I could get my own place where I could keep my altar private and hidden. To this day I always have at least two gris-gris in my purse for protection and love. —**Brandi Hudson**

Who is your favorite witch and why?
There are so many men and women I've met who are inspiring in their own magical ways. I'm constantly surprised at how many people I know practice some form of witchcraft/alchemy/spirituality and don't flaunt it. I would have to choose Phil Hine, Scott Cunningham, David Bowie, and Claire Boucher, because their style of expressing themselves is unpretentious and genuine, as is their aptitude at creating a magical reality without shunning the collective reality. —**Christiana Key**

My favorite witches are the women for women. The list includes anyone from the girls I have spent time with who are victims of acid attacks on the other side of the world who sought asylum in the USA and still exude strength and humor, to Susan B. Anthony, Kathleen Hanna, Tina Fey, and my very own sister, Mariam, who traveled to Afghanistan back in 2002 to meet with folks in the Constitutional Commission regarding approaches to women's rights in the new Afghan constitution. There is no shortage of them, deeming it impossible to pick favorites. —**Zohra Atash**

How do you feel about the increasing visibility of the witch in pop culture?
It's fantastic! I find it to be an important aspect of current (fourth-wave?) feminism. I also feel much more open about my alignment with witches and witchcraft. Maybe the other witches and witch lovers were always there, but I am finding them to be more and more visible in my life and the world around me. —**Katy Horan**

It really depends. Some of it I enjoy in a really kitschy way. The aesthete side of me digs it because those are the kinds of images I'm attracted to. That said, I feel the same way about it that

I felt when I was a teenager and a band I really loved blew up and then everybody liked them because it was fashionable, and you're like "No, but I really understand it and I really love it!" which is kind of an immature reaction. On the other hand, if these symbols are bubbling up in the collective unconscious right now, I do think it's for a reason, and I think they can really be a gateway for some people. Honestly, I think a lot of scholars don't like to admit it, but that's how they got into it in the first place, because they picked up a book or saw an image in a film that awakened something in them. So if this just means that some people are getting intrigued by it and it'll start them down a path to some real research and some real learning, I don't see anything wrong with that. —**Pam Grossman**

I believe there has always been a fascination with witches, even when Christians were burning them. I believe it is because of the sacred energy of the feminine and the power that resonates inside everyone who's ever been birthed. We all start as female, that should say a lot. There is a wealth of that information inside our cellular memory whether we like it or choose it. Everyone has the power to create and manipulate the world around them but the "witch" goes against the culturalization of relegating women to a subclass. How can you suppress a half of humanity without suppressing their most natural abilities? The more that women regain their power, the more the witch becomes a symbol of that regrowth. —**Paige A. Flash**

How do you feel about the popularity of witch fashion?
I have mixed feelings. On one hand, I've met so many inspiring women who manifest this one look. That's great. It's very bonding. Then again, certain big brands are using it in a very capitalist way, and only putting the clothes on white girls who are really skinny. If someone sees that and it prompts them to explore witchcraft then good on them, but the idea of men in these companies saying, "How can we capitalize on this new popular trend of being spooky?" bothers me. —**Elisabeth O'Driscoll**

What has practicing witchcraft taught you about female friendships and sisterhood?

There's something that happens naturally when you meet other women you feel connected to, and you want to gather and work throughout the seasons of the year for a common goal. It's that idea of sisterhood, coming together, the meeting of the minds. Let's combine our forces. At each stage of our womanhood we need to appreciate the moment and learn from the ones who are younger than us and older than us because we've all been there and we're all going there. It's about having a collective experience with people who go through some of the same experiences.—Cat Cabral

How does your practice of witchcraft impact your feminism and vice versa?

Part of living a magical life for me means I integrate my practice and ideals as a witch into every aspect of my life. I don't go to work and then come home and put on my witch hat. It's always there to varying degrees depending on circumstance. The resurgence of Goddess practices like the Goddess Movement and the Red Tent Movement are very much a rejection of the suppression of feminine energy, and so I personally see them as being political movements as well as spiritual. I also believe that the rejection of the gender binary is in many ways a product of the idea that feminine and masculine energy are present in all beings regardless of their physical biology. Goddess energy is available to everyone, and the feminine is rising.
—Vanessa Irena

Witchcraft and feminism entered my life around the same time—when I was nine. My friends and I were heavily obsessed with Sailor Moon and the Spice Girls, so when we learned about Wicca (saw *The Craft*) the admission was seamless. Witchcraft has always been about the power of love and friendship to me, and my feminism started that way too—by bonding with women. Now I see both more as a power of the

self and body, but it was through my coven that I learned this.
—Morgan Claire Sirene

I don't separate my witchcraft from my feminism—they're very much similar mechanics of my belief systems. For me, witchcraft and feminism share the same goal: self-sovereignty. I think this is why witchcraft has historically belonged to women and queer folx rather than men—it is intrinsically a means of rebellion against oppression and reclaiming stolen power. —Melissa Madara

What role does technology play in your witchcraft practice?
For me, technology is just another tool at my magickal disposal. If I can conjure spirits with an old root and a circle of salt, why not through a website? The world of magick has broadened and taken on new definitions alongside human advancement, and the incorporation of technology into the practice seems to be the next organic step. I use unique hashtags to communicate with my ancestors, I bless my phone and laptop before online dating, and I charge sigils through Instagram. As with any other tool in the hands of a witch, the possibilities are endless.
—Melissa Madara

What rituals or spells do you do to protect yourself?
Whenever I'm traveling or going somewhere on my own where I don't feel safe, I light candles and say a prayer to Santa Muerte for protection. I also carry a bunch of crystals, like Citrine, Onyx, and Bloodstone that help give me confidence and drive away darkness in my life, and I carry at least two images of La Virgen with me everywhere I go to provide extra protection. A lot of my casual spellwork is just preparing things that make me feel safe when I go out into the world. —Mey Rude

What are some of your favorite spells or remedies for opening the sacral chakra or fostering sexual energy?
Since the sacral chakra is associated with the color orange, orange crystals, fruits, and vegetables can be used for opening this

chakra. My absolute favorite fruit is mango, and mangos are associated with the sacral chakra. I also love carrot juice. Cinnamon is also associated with the sacral chakra, and is lovely in teas, oils and baked desserts. I recently made an infusion of mango and cinnamon in red wine for the first time. I'm realizing while answering this question that I made a sacral chakra remedy without even realizing it! Also, oatstraw increases sensitivity to pleasure, and jasmine is very sensual. —**Damali Abrams**

Oshun loves spells that involve sunflowers and honey. She is a very sexy and empowering goddess, always interested in making sure you get the job, making sure you look your best. To liven your sex life up or if you need to really break a dry spell, get a sunflower and put a drop of honey on it. Rub the sunflower over the front of your vulva and ask for empowerment within that chakra. Ask for that beauty and that sexual energy. When you're done you can throw the flower away in a plastic bag, but it's ideal to bury the flower if you have a yard. You can also work with any other similar goddess like Venus or Lakshmi. —**Sonia Ortiz**

Kundalini, Kundalini, Kundalini! I practice it both in yoga and in meditation. I stumbled onto kundalini while looking into different types of yoga classes. Around the same time, a friend gave me a kundalini meditation audio track. The concept was new to me and I had many thoughts going through my head reading and hearing about a coiled serpent and all of the purposeful ways it travels through my body, but nothing could actually prepare me for feeling my awareness and the physical response of my body the first time you feel that energy awaken and rise, hitting all your chakra points as it moves through you. It wasn't immediate, but happened for the first time one day during meditation totally by accident. Since then, I have preached it as not only an opener for those pathways to expression and creativity, but also for a better outlook on life. —**Paige A. Flash**

Start a small fire in your cauldron or light a large red candle to symbolize love, passion, joy, and fertility (in all senses of the word). Work your magic skyclad, or nude, and start your spell close to midnight. Put on some music that inspires ecstatic dancing and move wildly around your fire until you fall into a trance. When your energy is raised and your intent clear, send all of it into the fire, and when the moment feels right, jump over it. Working nude is preferred for fire safety and as an expression of healthy sexuality and love for one's beautiful body. If you have a partner, what a perfect ritual to share with your loved one and let the sparks ignite your passion deep into the night as the sun rises. —**Cat Cabral**

How has your witch identity or witchcraft practice impacted your life for the better?
Being a witch has always given me a fierce sense of individuality and self-confidence. Especially once I found *The Satanic Bible*. I feel like it opened my eyes to there being a lot of different ways to think in the world, and in trying times when I would have to cope with prejudice. After that, I really just felt bad for the close-minded plebeians who couldn't wrap their head around the idea of whatever they didn't like about me. Also let's be real, when daily bullshit pops up you know you can always conjure a little fix for it, so the problem doesn't seem to be as much of a problem. —**Severely Mame**

Witchcraft makes you work on your shit. It makes you think about the larger human family. It makes you want to be good to yourself so you can be good to others, and so they can be good to others. Witchcraft makes you believe in yourself and believe that you have something to offer the world. Instead of having that "who am I," "what can I do," "my vote doesn't count" view, witchcraft offers you power to change your life and to help change others. It's my responsibility. To me that's the closest you can get to God, in that you're responsible for life on this planet and you need to do what you can to help. —**Jaclyn Sheer**

WORKS CITED

Introduction

Slutist. www.slutist.com

Doll, Jen. "An A-to-Z Guide to 2012's Worst Words." *The Atlantic.* December 18, 2012.

Valenti, Jessica. "SlutWalks and the future of feminism." *The Washington Post.* June 3, 2011.

Rys, Dan. "Stevie Nicks Sees Women's Rights Slipping, 'And I Hate It.'" *Rolling Stone.* Mar 15, 2013.

Villarreal, Yvonne. "Stevie Nicks Talks 'American Horror Story': 'I Was Scared To Go There.'" *Los Angeles Times.* January 8, 2014.

Witches, Sluts, Feminists

Syfret, Wendy. "How We Became Generation Witch." *I-D.* January 14, 2016.

Crane, Susan. "Clothing and Gender Definition: Joan of Arc." *Journal of Medieval and Early Modern Studies*, vol. 26, issue 2, 1996.

Fandrich, Ina Johanna. 2014. *Marie Laveau, the Mysterious Voudou Queen: A Study of Powerful Female Leadership in Nineteenth-Century New Orleans.* London: Routledge.

Yousafzai, Malala. 2013. *I Am Malala: The Girl Who Stood Up for Education and Was Shot by the Taliban.* Boston: Little, Brown and Co.

hooks, bell. 2000. *Feminism Is for Everybody.* Cambridge: South End Press.

Jones, Malcolm. "The Surprising Roots of the Word 'Slut.'" *The Daily Beast.* March 21, 2015.

Liberman, Anatoly. "The Oxford Etymologist goes Trick-or-Treating." October 24, 2007.

"Witch." *Merriam-Webster.* www.m-w.com.

"Witch of Agnesi." Wolfram MathWorld. www.wolfram.mathworld.com.

Adler, Margot. 1979. *Drawing Down the Moon: Witches, Druids, Goddess-Worshippers, and Other Pagans in America Today.* Reprint. New York: Penguin, 1986.

Herstik, Gabriela. "Material World, Mystical Girl: The Hoodwitch." *The Numinous.* April 26, 2016.

Cabot, Laurie and Jean Mills. 1997. *The Witch in Every Woman.* New York: Delta.

Grossman, Pam. 2016. *What Is a Witch* Illus. Tin Can Forest. Toronto: Tin Can Forest Press.

Witch Slut Are You? The Medieval to the Modern

Sjoo, Monica and Barbara Mor. 1987. *The Great Cosmic Mother: Rediscovering the Religion of the Earth.* San Francisco: Harper and Row.

Eisler, Riane. 1987. *The Chalice and the Blade: Our History, Our Future*. New York: Harper Collins.

King James Bible Online. www.kingjamesbibleonline.org.

Demos, John. 2008. *The Enemy Within: A Short History of Witch-Hunting*. New York: Penguin.

Kramer, Heinrich and Jacob Sprenger. 1971. *The Malleus Maleficarum*. Translated by Montague Summers. London: Arrow.

Mackay, Christopher S. 2009. *The Hammer of Witches: A Complete Translation of the Malleus Maleficarum*. Cambridge: Cambridge UP.

Smith, Moira. "The Flying Phallus and the Laughing Inquisitor: Penis Theft in the 'Malleus Maleficarum.'" *Journal of Folklore Research*, vol. 39, no. 1, 2002, pp. 85-117.

Schuyler, Jane. "The 'Malleus Maleficarum' and Baldung's 'Witches' Sabbath.'" *Notes in the History of Art*, vol. 6, no. 3, 1987, pp. 20-26.

Hults, Linda C. 2011. *The Witch As Muse: Art, Gender, and Power in Early Modern Europe*. Philadelphia: U Penn Press.

Roper, Lyndal. 2004. *Witch Craze: Terror and Fantasy in Baroque Germany*. New Haven: Yale UP.

Barstow, Anne Llewellyn. 1994. *Witchcraze: A New History of the European Witch Hunts*. New York: HarperOne.

Ehrenreich, Barbara and Deirdre English. 2014. *Witches, Midwives, and Nurses: A History of Women Healers*. 2nd ed. New York: Feminist Press.

Garvey, Megan. "Transcript of the disturbing video 'Elliot Rodger's Retribution.'" *Los Angeles Times*. May 24, 2014.

Fard, Maggie Fazeli. "Sandra Fluke, Georgetown student called a 'slut' by Rush Limbaugh, speaks out." *The Washington Post*. March 2, 2012.

ABC News. "Rush Limbaugh Calls a Female Georgetown Student, Sandra Fluke, a 'Slut.'" Online video clip. *YouTube*. March 6, 2012.

"Amber Rose." *Instagram*. www.instagram.com/amberrose.

Valenti, Jessica. "What makes a slut? The only rule, it seems, is being female." *The Guardian*. June 23, 2014.

Gibson, Megan. "Study: Women Slut-Shame Each Other on Twitter as Much as Men Do." *Time*. May 21, 2014.

Hess, Amanda. "Slut-Shaming Isn't Just a 'Girl-On-Girl' Crime." *Slate*. June 7, 2013.

Hackman, Rose. "Amber Rose interview: Even when I was a virgin, I was called a slut." *The Guardian*. November 3, 2015.

Pilkington, Ed. "SlutWalking gets rolling after cop's loose talk about provocative clothing." *The Guardian*. May 6, 2011.

Buchwald, Emilie, et al., eds. 1993. *Transforming a Rape Culture*. Minneapolis: Milkweed Editions.

All-American Witch: Salem's Legacy

"Wingwoman." *Inside Amy Schumer*, season 3, episode 9, HBO, June 30, 2015.

Schiff, Stacy. 2015. *The Witches: Salem, 1692*. New York: Little, Brown & Co.

Howe, Katherine, ed. 2014. *The Penguin Book of Witches*. New York: Penguin.

Karlsen, Carol F. 1998. *The Devil in the Shape of a Woman: Witchcraft in Colonial New England*. New York: Norton.

Mappen, Marc, ed. 2002. *Witches & Historians: Interpretations of Salem*. Malabar, FL: Krieger Publishing Co.

The Midwife: Bestial Bodies & Reproductive Rights

Bourdillon, Hilary. 1989. *Women as Healers: A History of Women and Medicine*. Cambridge: Cambridge UP.

Reagan, Leslie J. 1998. *When Abortion Was a Crime: Women, Medicine, and Law in the United States, 1867-1973*. Berkeley: U of California Press.

Scherer, Michael. "Rick Santorum Wants to Fight 'The Dangers of Contraception.'" *Time*. February 14, 2012.

Moore, Lori. "Rep. Todd Akin: The Statement and the Reaction." *The New York Times*. August 20, 2012.

Marcotte, Amanda. "Idaho Lawmaker Who Doesn't Understand Female Anatomy Knows What's Good for Women." *Slate*. February 24, 2015.

"The Planned Parenthood witch hunt." *The Washington Post*. February 20, 2016.

Rumpf, Sarah. "Rick Perry: Planned Parenthood 'Profits Off the Tragedy of a Destroyed Human Life.'" *Breitbart News*. July 15, 2015.

Lee, Michelle Ye Hee. "For Planned Parenthood abortion stats, '3 percent' and '94 percent' are both misleading." *The Washington Post*. August 12, 2015.

Harris, Gardiner. "Obama Vetoes Bill to Repeal Health Law and End Planned Parenthood Funding." *The New York Times*. January 8, 2016.

Sun, Lena H. "Obama officials warn states about cutting Medicaid funds to Planned Parenthood." *The Washington Post*. April 19, 2016.

Flegenheimer, Matt and Maggie Haberman. "Donald Trump, Abortion Foe, Eyes 'Punishment' For Women, Then Recants." *The New York Times*. March 30, 2016.

Garcia, Feliks. "Mike Pence once said condoms are 'very poor' defense against STDs." *The Independent*. July 21, 2016.

Mehta, Seema. "Roe vs. Wade will be overturned if Donald Trump wins, Mike Pence says." *Los Angeles Times*. July 29, 2016.

Federici, Silvia. 2004. *Caliban and the Witch: Women, the Body and Primitive Accumulation*. New York: Autonomedia.

Political Witch: Rebellion & Revolution

The Satanic Temple of Detroit. "The Satanic Temple of Detroit – Sanctions of the Cross." Online video clip. *YouTube*. March 25, 2016.

"Our Mission." *The Satanic Temple*. www.thesatanictemple.com.

The Satanic Temple of Detroit. "Women's Health Initiatives." www.thesatanictempledetroit.com.

The Sabbat Cycle. www.sabbatcycle.com.

Allen, Samantha. "Michigan Satanists Defend Planned Parenthood on Good Friday." *The Daily Beast*. March 25, 2016.

The Wizard of Oz. Directed by Victor Fleming, Metro-Goldwyn-Mayer, 1939.

Goldsmith, Barbara. 1999. *Other Powers: The Age of Suffrage, Spiritualism, and the Scandalous Victoria Woodhull*. New York: Harper Perennial.

Rappaport, Helen. "Sojourner Truth." *Encyclopedia of Women Social Reformers*. Santa Barbara: ABC CLIO, 2001.

Painter, Nell Irvin. "Sojourner Truth's Religion in Her Moment of Pentecostalism and Witchcraft." *Spellbound: Women and Witchcraft in America*, edited by Elizabeth Reis. Wilmington, DE: Scholarly Resources, 1998.

Gabriel, Mary. 1998. *Notorious Victoria: The Life of Victoria Woodhull, Uncensored*. New York City: Algonquin Books.

Lenz, Lyz. "America's Scandalous, Psychic, Forgotten First Female Presidential Candidate." *Broadly*. February 11, 2016.

Boland, Sue. "'Wicked' History." *The Post-Standard*. February 2, 2010.

Gage, Matilda Joslyn. 1893. *Woman, Church and State*. Reprint. Watertown, MA: Persephone Press, 1980.

Morgan, Robin, ed. 1970. *Sisterhood Is Powerful: An Anthology of Writings from the Women's Liberation Movement*. New York: Vintage.

Echols, Alice. 1989. *Daring to Be Bad: Radical Feminism in America 1967-1975*. Minneapolis: U of Minnesota Press.

Morgan, Robin. 1978. *Going Too Far: The Personal Chronicle of a Feminist*. New York: Random House.

Bradley, Patricia. 2004. *Mass Media and the Shaping of American Feminism, 1963-1975*. Jackson: U. of Mississippi.

Ephron, Nora. "Women." *Esquire*. November 1972.

Hillary Clinton: Wicked Witch of the Left

John Dennis 2010. "Nancy Pelosi, Wicked Witch of the West." Online video clip. *YouTube*. September 12, 2010.

"Ann Coulter Gets Torn to Pieces at Rob Lowe's Roast. Grab The Popcorn." *Queerty*. August 30, 2016.

North, Anna. "The Witching Season." *The New York Times*. October 22, 2016.

Lee, Jasmine C. and Kevin Quealy. "The 282 People, Places and Things Donald Trump Has Insulted on Twitter: A Complete List." *The New York Times*. October 23, 2016.

Lazarro, Sage. "Women Are Trolling Conservatives by Trading in Their To-Do Lists for 'Vagendas.'" *Observer*. August 25, 2016.

McCann, Erin and Jonah Engel Bromwich. "'Nasty Woman' and 'Bad Hombres': The Real Debate Winners?" *The New York Times*. October 20, 2016.

Trumble, David. "Bern the Witch-Hunters." *The Huffington Post*. February 3, 2016.

Roudman, Sam. "'Bern the Witch' Sanders Supporter Speaks Out." *Vocativ*. March 11, 2016.

Raw Story. "Antonio Sabàto, J.: Give Hillary a 'broom so she can fly away, that witch.'" Online video clip. *YouTube.* July 6, 2016.

Hensch, Mark. "Limbaugh: Clinton 'a witch with a capital B.'" *The Hill.* September 27, 2016.

Reynolds, Christina. "A Witch Hunt." *Hillary for America.* Email. Received by Kristen Sollée, July 20, 2016.

Marcotte, Amanda. "Kudos to Hillary for playing the woman card: If people are going to call her a witch, she'll tell them she's Hermione Granger." *Salon.* July 29, 2016.

Reinhard, Beth and Janet Hook. "Donald Trump Says 'Second Amendment People' Can Stop Hillary Clinton from Curbing Gun Rights." *The Wall Street Journal.* August 10, 2016.

Gajanan, Mahita. "Donald Trump Just Called Hillary Clinton the Devil and Threatened to Prosecute Her." *Fortune.* October 9, 2016.

Krieg, Gregory. "It's Official: Clinton Swamps Trump in Popular Vote." *CNN.* December 22, 2016.

Samakow, Jessica. "This Election Showed Men How Our Country Has Always Treated Women." The *Huffington Post.* November 11, 2016.

West, Lindy. "Her Loss." *The New York Times.* November 11, 2016.

Sollée, Kristen. "Feminist Witches March For Women's Rights Across the Country." *Bustle.* January 23, 2017.

Vatomsky, Sonya. "W.I.T.C.H. PDX: Portland Brings Back the Women's International Terrorist Conspiracy From Hell." *Haute Macabre.* January 27, 2017.

Art Witch: Wanton Woodcuts & Domestic Goddesses

Kwan, Natalie. "Woodcuts and Witches: Ulrich Molitor's De lamiis et pythonicis mulieribus, 1489-1669." *German History,* vol. 30, issue 4, December 2012.

Grien, Hans Baldung. "Standing Witch with Monster." 1515, painting.

Guazzo, Francesco Maria. 1608. *Compendium Maleficarum.* Italy.

Falero, Luis Ricardo. "Witches Going to Their Sabbath." 1878, oil on canvas.

Berger, John. 1972. *Ways of Seeing.* Reprint. London: Penguin, 1990.

Ghost Bitch USA

"Ghost Bitch USA." *Freight + Volume Gallery,* New York, July 14–September 11, 2016.

Hassan, Carma et al., "Sandra Bland's family settles for $1.9M in wrongful death suit." *CNN.* September 15, 2016.

Tituba's Legacy

Condé, Maryse. 2009. *I, Tituba, Black Witch of Salem.* Trans. Richard Philcox. Charlottesville: U of Virginia.

Crenshaw, Kimberlé Williams. "Mapping the Margins: Intersectionality, Identity Politics, and Violence Against Women of Color." *The Public Nature of*

Private Violence, edited by Martha Fineman and Roxanne Mykitiuk. New York: Routledge, 1994.

Kendall, Mikki. "#SolidarityIsForWhiteWomen: women of color's issue with digital feminism." *The Guardian*. August 14, 2013.

Twitch of the Tongue: Language as Spell

Kamensky, Jane. "Female Speech and Other Demons: Witchcraft and Wordcraft in Early New England." *Spellbound: Women and Witchcraft in America*, edited by Elizabeth Reis. Wilmington, DE: Scholarly Resources, 1998.

Friedman, Ann. "Can We Just, Like, Get Over the Way Women Talk?" *New York Magazine*. July 9, 2015.

Tanenbaum, Leora. "What Does 'Slut' Mean, Anyway?" *The Huffington Post*. February 20, 2015.

West, Carolyn. "Mammy, Jezebel, Sapphire, and Their Homegirls: Developing an 'Oppositional Gaze' Towards the Image of Black Women." J. Chrisler et al., eds. *Lectures on the Psychology of Women*. New York: McGraw Hill, 2008.

Lutze, B. "Why I won't call myself a 'slut'." *Salon*. October 22, 2013.

Korvette, Kristen. "May Slut of the Month: Ev'Yan Whitney." *Slutist*. May 5, 2016.

Korvette, Kristen. "April Slut of the Month: Pilar Reyes." *Slutist*. March 31, 2015.

Korvette, Kristen. "April Slut of the Month: Emily Tepper." *Slutist*. April 11, 2013.

Johnson, Sunni. "August Slut of the Month: Lexi Laphor." *Slutist*. August 24, 2015.

Korvette, Kristen. "May Slut of the Month: Bunny Buxom." *Slutist*. April 28, 2015.

Damn, Josh. "Slutism: Mmh Yes." *Slutist*. April 29, 2013.

Starhawk. 1979. *The Spiral Dance: A Rebirth of the Ancient Religion of the Great Goddess*. Reprint. New York: HarperOne, 1999.

Cabot, Laurie, and Jean Mills. 1997. *The Witch in Every Woman*. New York: Delta.

Daly, Mary. 1978. *Gyn/Ecology: The Metaethics of Radical Feminism*. Reprint. Boston: Beacon Press, 1990.

Butler, Judith. 1997. *Excitable Speech: A Politics of the Performative*. New York: Routledge.

Kitt. "Taking The Sting out of S/M." *Coming to Power*, edited by Samois. 1981. Reprint. Boston: Alyson Publications, 1987.

Sollée, Kristen. "4 Vital Tips For Feminist Artists Creating In Trump's America." *Bustle*. January 31, 2017.

Webbe, George. 1619. *The Arraignement of an Unruly Tongue*. London.

Sex Magic & the Tools of Pleasure

Miklos, Vincze. "The Most Frightening Witches in Art History." *i09*. November 12, 2014.

Seymour, John Drelincourt. 2010. *Dame Alice Kyteler The Sorceress of Kilkenny A.D. 1324*. London: Pierides Press.

Molitor, Ulrich. 1489. *On witches and female soothsayers*. Germany. 1489.

Dürer, Albrecht. "Witch Riding Backwards on a Goat, with four putti carrying an alchemist's pot, a thorn apple plant." c.1500, engraving.

Cavendish, Richard. 1968. *The Black Arts: A Concise History of Witchcraft, Demonology, Astrology, and Other Mystical Practices throughout the Ages*. Reprint. London: Tarcher, 1983.

Pollan, Michael. 2002.*The Botany of Desire: A Plant's-Eye View of the World*. New York: Random House.

Anand, Margot. 1996. *The Art of Sexual Magic: Cultivating Sexual Energy to Transform Your Life*. London: Tarcher.

Chakrubs. www.chakrubs.com

Kinsey Institute. www.kinseyinstitute.org

Vagianos, Alanna. "13 Reasons Every Woman Should Masturbate Regularly." *The Huffington Post*. January 14, 2015.

The Spell of Seduction: Sex Work & the Sacred Whore

Q., Siouxsie. "The Whore Next Door: The Feminine Divine." *SF Weekly*. December 23, 2015.

Sex Workers Outreach Project. www.swopusa.org

Stone, Merlin. 1978. *When God Was a Woman*. New York: Mariner Books.

Rawlinson, George, trans. 1862. *History of Herodotus*. London: John Murray.

Queering the Witch: Porn, Pleasure & Representation

Grien, Hans Baldung. "New Year's Wish with Three Witches." c.1514, drawing.

Velasco, Sherry. 2011. *Lesbians in Early Modern Spain*. Nashville: Vanderbilt U. Press.

Ziv, Amalia. 2015. *Explicit Utopias: Rewriting the Sexual in Women's Pornography*. New York: SUNY Press.

Candida Royalle. www.candidaroyalle.com

Susie Bright. www.susiebright.blogs.com

Annie Sprinkle. www.anniesprinkle.org

Sollée, Kristen. "6 Sex-Positive Feminist Pioneers You Should Know About." *Bustle*. September 14, 2015.

Bussel, Rachel Kramer. "Organic, Fair-Trade Porn: On the Hunt for Ethical Smut." *The Daily Beast*. April 13, 2013.

Ward, Jane. "Queer Feminist Pigs: A Spectator's Manifesta." *The Feminist Porn Book: The Politics of Producing Pleasure*, edited by Tristan Taormino et al. New York: Feminist Press, 2013.

Louv, Jason. "Sex, the Occult, and the Witches Who Do Porn." *Motherboard*. November 1, 2013.

Vatomsky, Sonya. "Stripper with a PhD: Dirge Interviews Lux ATL." *Dirge Magazine*. July 13, 2016.

Paquette, Danielle. "President Obama just said we shouldn't shame women for having sex." *The Washington Post*. June 14, 2014.

Obama, Barack. "*Glamour* Exclusive: President Barack Obama Says, 'This Is What a Feminist Looks Like.'" *Glamour*. August 4, 2016.

Undressing the Witch: Fashion, Style & Sartorial Spells

Frankel, Susannah. "Rei Kawakubo: Fashion's Great Iconoclast." *Dazed*. Sept. 2004.

Hainey, Michael. "The Marquis de Sex." *GQ*. October 31, 2004.

Breslaw, Elaine G. 1995. *Tituba, Reluctant Witch of Salem: Devilish Indians and Puritan Fantasies*. New York: NYU Press.

Sterling, Alinor C. "Undressing the Victim: The Intersection of Evidentiary and Semiotic Meanings of Women's Clothing in Rape Trials." *Yale Journal of Law & Feminism*, vol. 7, issue 1, 1995.

Mendes, Kaitlynn. 2015. *SlutWalk: Feminism, Activism and Media*. New York: Palgrave Macmillan.

Lau, Susie. "Up close with Comme des Garçons coven of witches." *Dazed*. 2015.

Menkes, Suzy. "A Modest Proposal." *T Magazine*. March 19, 2013.

Witchcraft On Screen: Living Deliciously

The Love Witch. Directed by Anna Biller, Anna Biller, 2016.

The Witch. Directed by Robert Eggers, A24, 2015.

Creed, Barbara. 1993. *The Monstrous-Feminine: Film, Feminism, Psychoanalysis*. New York: Routledge.

Häxan. Directed by Benjamin Christensen, Svensk Filmindustri, 1922.

Snow White and the Seven Dwarfs. Directed by David Hand, Walt Disney Productions, 1937.

Sleeping Beauty. Directed by Clyde Geronimi, Walt Disney Productions, 1959.

Black Sunday. Directed by Mario Bava, Galatea Film, 1960.

Friedan, Betty. 1963. *The Feminine Mystique*. New York: Norton.

"I, Darrin, Take This Witch, Samantha." *Bewitched*, written by Sol Saks, directed by William Asher, Screen Gems, 1964.

The Witches of Eastwick. Directed by George Miller, Warner Bros., 1987.

The Craft. Directed by Andrew Fleming, Columbia Pictures, 1996.

Sirene, Morgan Claire. "Poisonous Nostalgia: A Pagan Witch's Guide to Burying 'The Craft' Cult." *Slutist*. August 17, 2015.

Weiss, Suzannah. "This Is What *Harry Potter* Titles Would Look Like If Hermione Got the Credit She Deserves." *Refinery 29*. December 23, 2016.

Maleficent. Directed by Robert Stromberg, Walt Disney Studios, 2014.

"Interview With Anna Biller, Director of *The Love Witch*." *New Jack Witch*. January 2, 2017.

Rife, Katie. "*The Witch* Director Robert Eggers on Fellini, Feminism, and Period-Accurate Candlelight." *A.V. Club*. February 23, 2016.

The Coven: Crafting Feminist Community
Ongley, Hannah. "The secret online girl cult trying to unseat the Stanford rape judge." *i-D*. June 13, 2016.
"Under Coven: The Witches of Bushwick." *Broadly*. Online video clip. October 26, 2015.
Korvette, Kristen. "Lizz Winstead: The First Lady of Political Satire Talks Protest, Fake News, and Feminist Party Jams." *Slutist*. January 19, 2017.
Korvette, Kristen. "Conjuring Community With Brooklyn's Ravenous Craft." *Slutist*. March 9, 2016.

Music Witch: Sound as Sorcery
Tweedle, Sam. "This Week at PCA: Jinx Dawson." *Confessions of a Pop Culture Addict*. November 7, 2014.
Zoladz, Lindsay. "Yoko Ono and the Myth That Deserves to Die." *Vulture*. May 13, 2015.
Yoko Ono. "Yes, I'm a Witch." *A Story*, Rykodisc, 1974.
Rogers, Ray. "A Storm Called Stevie." *Interview*. July 1998.
Koren, Oriana. "Beyoncé's 'Lemonade' Is the Epitome of Black Girl Magic." *The Establishment*. April 28, 2016.
Mayard, Judnick. "Beyoncé Brings Wonderful Witchcraft, Healing Powers in 'Lemonade.'" *Billboard*. April 29, 2016.
Hobson, Janell. "Lemonade: Beyoncé's Redemption Song." *Ms. Magazine*. April 29, 2016.
Stevens, Kenya K. "The Metaphysics of Lemonade and Beyoncé's Polyamory." *JujuMama*. May 2,2016.
Doyle, Sady. "Season of the Witch: Why Young Women Are Flocking to the Ancient Craft." *The Guardian*. February 24, 2015.
Azizaa Aaziza. "Black Magic Woman." Online video clip. *YouTube*. August 21, 2015.
Lebrave, Benjamin. "Azizaa Is Challenging Christianity's Grip Ghana." *The Fader*. September 2 2015.
Korvette, Kristen. "June Slut of the Month: Christiana Key." *Slutist*. May 28, 2013.
Potts, Dianca London. "Slutist's Legacy of the Witch Fest Was a NSFW Celebration of the Feminine and the Divine." *Noisey*. April 27, 2016.

Hex Sells: Feminism, Capitalism & the Witch
"15 Urban Outfitters controversies." *The Week*. April 29, 2016.
Califia, Pat. "Damned in the USA." *Skin Two*. Issue 13, 1993.
Zeisler, Andi. 2016. *We Were Feminists Once: From Riot Grrrl to CoverGirl, The Buying and Selling of a Political Movement*. New York: PublicAffairs.

hooks, bell. "Dig Deep: Beyond Lean In." *The Feminist Wire*. October 28, 2013.

Boycott, Rosie. "Scandal of the 62p-an-hour T-shirts: Shame on the feminists who betrayed the cause." *Daily Mail*. November 8, 2014.

Kale, Sirin. "How Much It Sucks to Be a Sri Lankan Worker Making Beyoncé's New Clothing Line." *Broadly*. May 17, 2016.

Moore, Anne Elizabeth. 2016. *Threadbare: Clothes, Sex & Trafficking*. Portland: Microcosm Publishing.

Tech Witch: Online Activism & the Digital Mystic

Darcy, Dame. 1994. *Handbook for Hot Witches: Dame Darcy's Illustrated Guide to Magic, Love, & Creativity*. New York: Henry Holt & Co.

Fernandez, Maria et al., ed. 2003. *Domain Errors!: Cyberfeminist Practices*. Brooklyn: Autonomedia.

Kolko, Beth et al., eds. 2000. *Race in Cyberspace*. London: Routledge.

Duggan, Maeve. "Part 1: Experiencing Online Harassment." *Pew Research*. October 22, 2014.

Dewey, Caitlin. "Every 10 seconds, someone on Twitter calls a woman a 'slut' or 'whore.'" *The Washington Post*. May 26, 2016.

Barksdale, Aaron. "18 Times Black Twitter Broke the Internet in 2015." *The Huffington Post*. December 10, 2015.

Blay, Zeba. "21 Hashtags That Changed the Way We Talk about Feminism." *The Huffington Post*. March 21, 2016.

Song, Sandra. "Banish Internet Trolls with Spells from Molly Soda's Virtual Spellbook." *Paper*. July 27, 2015.

Towers, Tarin. "How to Cast Spells Using Emoji." *Broadly*. October 29, 2015.

Yeni Sleidi. "Brujas Hex Trump." Online video clip. *YouTube*. September 10, 2015.

Paul, Kari. "Hundreds of Witches Just Hexed Stanford Rapist Brock Turner." *Broadly*. June 9, 2016.

Saxena, Jaya. "Witches put a hex on Martin Shkreli—and it might be working." *The Daily Dot*. March 3, 2016.

Yerbamala Collective. "Our Vendetta: Witches vs Fascists." https://drive.google.com/file/d/0B2mqLg0R-Yc1NE9DQ3FGN3dqQkE/view

Sipress, Jaliessa. "Witches Under Empire: What It Means To Be a Witch in 'Trump's America.'" *The Hoodwitch*. January 30, 2017.

Parton, Heather Digby. "Building the Realm of Alternative Facts: Trump's Lies Are Enabled by Years of Right-Wing Media." *Salon*. February 6, 2017.

Leonhardt, David. "Trump Flirts With Theocracy." *The New York Times*. January 30, 2017.

The Legacy of the Witch

Gay, Roxane. "Unruly Women Are Always Witches: Outlander S1 E10." *The Toast*. April 18, 2015.

Castleman, Michael. "'Hysteria' and the Strange History of Vibrators." *Psychology Today*. March 1, 2013.

Maines, Rachel P. 2001. *The Technology of Orgasm: 'Hysteria,' the Vibrator, and Women's Sexual Satisfaction*. Baltimore: Johns Hopkins UP.

Epure, Ioana. "The Women of Ghana's Witch Camps." *Broadly*. February 1, 2016.

Barnett, Errol. "Witchcraft in Tanzania: The good, bad and the persecution." *CNN*. October 8, 2012.

Singh, Vikram. "India's Deadly Superstition." *The New York Times*. Online video clip. February 24, 2015.

Russell, Kent. "They Burn Witches Here." *The Huffington Post*. October 29, 2015.

Rann, Max. "Women Not Witches: Meet the People Fighting Sorcery Attacks in Papua New Guinea." *Vice*. February 13, 2015.

Biswas, Soutik. "The Indian woman who hunts the witch hunters." *BBC News*. April 10, 2016.

Kim, Meeri. "Study finds that fear can travel quickly through generations of mice DNA." *The Washington Post*. December 7, 2013.

Rodriguez, Tori. "Descendants of Holocaust Survivors Have Altered Stress Hormones." *Scientific American*. March 1, 2015.

Walsh, Kate et al., eds. "Mechanisms Underlying Sexual Violence Exposure and Psychosocial Sequelae: A Theoretical and Empirical Review." *Clinical Psychology: Science and Practice*, vol. 19, issue 3, Sept. 2012.

Smith, Darron T., PhD. "The Epigenetics of Being Black and Feeling Blue: Understanding African American Vulnerability to Disease." *The Huffington Post*. October 14, 2013.

Starhawk. www.Starhawk.org

ACKNOWLEDGMENTS

This book is dedicated to all the women—past and present—who have been demonized, persecuted, and denigrated, and to all those who have used their magic to fight back. It could not have been written without the family, friends, and cohorts who continually inspire me with their advocacy, open-heartedness, intelligence, and creative brilliance. The following are just a few of the people and groups who helped conjure this primer into being and deserve a shout-out:

My mother, for guiding me with her boundless gifts of intuition, empathy, and precision on the page.

My father, for cultivating my love of learning and instilling a healthy sense of skepticism in me.

Charlie, for being my ride or die, and supporting my wild nature whatever the cost.

Morgan, for tirelessly reading countless drafts, offering incomparably incisive edits, and renewing my faith in the boundless beauty of femme collaboration.

Tina, for planting the seed for this book, midwifing it to fruition, and teaching me so much about my craft along the way.

Anthony, for conjuring my visions into vivid aesthetic expressions that always surpass my expectations.

Judy, for lending essential legal and logical expertise as an editor.

Dianne, for channeling the spirits to aid in my process, and giving the gift of healing.

Lila, for always encouraging me to be bolder, and for being the very first *Slutist* supporter.

Ivan, for offering invaluable critiques and advice that have impacted my writing and thinking since college.

The New School and Eugene Lang College, for allowing me to share this interdisciplinary subject with young minds, and my students for edifying and challenging me.

Saint Vitus, for generously opening up their decadent

locale for my festival every year and always making me feel at home.

The following whip-smart witches, for providing support and (s)inspiration in my creative process: Sandra, Sybil, Jacq, Darcey, Naomi, Elena, Justina, and Kindra.

And most of all, to the artists, activists, witches, and scholars cited in this book—I am forever indebted to you for making such powerful contributions to this narrative.